Academic Writing for International Students of Business

International students of Business or Economics often need to write essays and reports for exams and coursework, and this new, second edition of *Academic Writing for International Students of Business* has been completely revised and updated to help them succeed with these tasks.

This book explains the academic writing process from start to finish, and practises all the key writing skills in the context of Business Studies. The book can be used either with a teacher or for self-study, and is clearly organised into four parts, with each divided into short units that contain examples, explanations and exercises for use in the classroom or for self-study:

1   **The Writing Process**, from assessing sources to proofreading
2   **Elements of Writing**, practising skills such as making comparisons
3   **Vocabulary for Writing**, dealing with areas such as nouns and adjectives, adverbs and verbs, synonyms, prefixes and prepositions, in an academic context
4   **Writing Models**, illustrating case studies, reports, longer essays and other key genres

This is an up-to-date book that reflects the interests and issues of contemporary Business Studies, with revised exercises, updated reading texts and a new glossary to ensure accessibility and maximise usability. Students wanting to expand their academic potential will find this practical and easy-to-use book an invaluable guide to writing in English for their degree courses, and it will also help students planning a career with international companies or organisations, where proficiency in written English is a key skill.

- All aspects of writing clearly explained, with full glossary for reference
- Full range of practice exercises, with answer key included
- Use of authentic academic texts
- Fully updated, with sections on finding electronic sources and evaluating internet material

Stephen Bailey is a freelance writer of materials for English for Academic Purposes. He has taught students in Barcelona, Tokyo, Johor Bahru, Prague and Toulouse, and more recently in the UK at Derby University and the University of Nottingham. His other books include *Academic Writing: A Handbook for International Students* (Routledge) and *Heartlands: A Guide to D. H. Lawrence's Midlands Roots* (with Chris Nottingham) (Matador).

Academic Writing for International Students of Business

Second edition

Stephen Bailey

 Routledge
Taylor & Francis Group

LONDON AND NEW YORK

Second edition published 2015
by Routledge
2 Park Square, Milton Park, Abingdon, Oxon OX14 4RN

and by Routledge
711 Third Avenue, New York NY 10017

Routledge is an imprint of the Taylor & Francis Group, an informa business

First edition published 2011 by Routledge

British Library Cataloguing in Publication Data
A catalogue record for this book is available from the British Library

Library of Congress Cataloging in Publication Data
Bailey, Stephen, 1947–
Academic writing for international students of business/
Stephen Bailey. – 2nd Edition.
pages cm
Previous ed.: 1st ed., 2011.
Includes bibliographical references and index.
1. Authorship. 2. Academic writing. 3. Business writing. I. Title.
PN151.B26 2015
808.02 – dc23
2014030152

ISBN: 978-1-138-78389-8 (hbk)
ISBN: 978-1-138-78390-4 (pbk)
ISBN: 978-1-315-76843-4 (ebk)

Typeset in Galliard
by Florence Production Ltd, Stoodleigh, Devon, UK

Printed and bound in Great Britain by
TJ International Ltd, Padstow, Cornwall

Contents

Part 1
The Writing Process

Acknowledgements

I would like to thank the many students I have taught over the past 30 years, whose needs have provided the impetus for this book. Their enthusiasm and resilience has been a constant inspiration for me.

My wife Rene has provided me with invaluable support, encouragement and advice on many aspects of academic writing during the development of this book. Final thanks are due to my daughter, Sophie, for helping me to keep the whole subject in perspective!

Introduction for Teachers

This course has been developed to help international students of Business and Economics with their writing assignments in English, at both undergraduate and postgraduate level. There is significant research (e.g. Bacha and Bahous, 2008) to suggest that such students tend to underestimate the difficulty of completing these tasks, in terms of both the reading and writing skills involved.

In addition, lecturers at Nottingham University Business School, Nottingham Business School, Birmingham Business School and Manchester Business School have shared their concerns with me about the writing challenges faced by their international students. These focus on difficulties with vocabulary, and the lack of critical thinking skills, with regard to reading and writing. Concern was also felt about students' failure to answer the specific question and their inability to develop answers logically. Issues around plagiarism and referencing skills are also significant worries.

The second edition of *Academic Writing for International Students of Business* sets out to address these and other problems directly. Although the trend towards the internationalisation of Business courses has substantial benefits, and international students are not expected to write perfect English, it should be understood that accurate and effective language use is an essential skill for such students. What may be individually minor problems with prepositions, word endings, spelling and articles can result in essays that are barely comprehensible to the best-motivated marker.

This book has been designed for use both in the classroom and for self-study/reference. This is a recognition that foundation, in-sessional and pre-sessional courses are inevitably time-constrained, and that some students may prefer or need to work by themselves. All exercises can be done individually or in pairs and groups. Students can check their work using the answer key. The book is designed for ease of access and simplicity of reference, which is achieved via the structure:

Part	Topic	Main application
1	**The Writing Process** from analysing titles to proofreading	Classroom use
2	**Elements of Writing** from argument to presenting visual information	Classroom use and self-study
3	**Vocabulary for Writing** from abbreviations to synonyms	Classroom use, self-study and reference
4	**Writing Models** from case studies to surveys	Classroom use, self-study and reference
	Answers	

Students are guided through the stages of the writing process in Part 1 and then the related writing skills are explained and practised in Part 2. Part 3 is designed to assist students with aspects of academic vocabulary, understandably a prime concern for many non-native users of English. Part 4 provides models of some common writing formats such as case studies. Cross-references are included to help students find relevant material, in this format:

▶ **See Unit 2.13 Style**

Teachers may wish to work through the writing process in Part 1 while referring to units in Part 2 as the group progresses. (Part 2 is not intended to be taught from start to finish: note the alphabetical organisation of Parts 2, 3 and 4). Revision exercises are provided at the end of Parts 1, 2 and 4.

The material in this course has been extensively tested in the classroom, but improvements can always be achieved in future editions. Therefore, I would be very glad to receive any comments or suggestions about the book from teachers of Business, Economics or English for Academic Purposes.

Stephen Bailey
Email: stephen.bailey@w3z.co.uk

Reference

Bacha, N. and Bahous, R. (2008) 'Contrasting views of business students' writing needs in an EFL environment'. *English for Specific Purposes* 27, 1, 74–93.

Introduction for Students

Why is writing English more difficult than speaking?

Many international students who arrive at college to study in English can speak the language well enough for normal life: shopping, travelling and meeting people. But the same students are often surprised to find that writing essays and reports in English is much more difficult. It can be helpful to think about the reasons for this situation.

First, speaking is usually done face to face. If your listener can't understand you, then they can look puzzled and ask you to repeat. But this doesn't work with a reader! When we write, we usually have little idea who may read our work, so we have to write as clearly as possible so that it is easy to understand.

With academic writing, writers and readers have to learn special conventions, such as using capital letters in certain places. If you do not follow these conventions, your meaning may be unclear and your teacher can have difficulty assessing your work. Another issue is vocabulary. Most academic subjects require writers to use semi-formal language, which is different from the idiomatic language used in speech. One example is using a verb such as 'continue' instead of phrasal verbs such as 'go on'.

What is the purpose of the book?

This book is designed to help you succeed in the writing tasks you may be given as part of your Business or Economics course. The kind of work that you are given may be different from the work you have done before, and this may be the first time you have had to write long essays or reports in English.

Your teachers know that English is not your native language and will be sympathetic to the problems you have in your writing. But at the same time, you will want to learn to write as clearly and accurately as possible not only to succeed on your current course, but also in preparation for your career. Almost all large companies and organisations expect their staff to be able to communicate effectively in written English, as well as orally. Therefore, during your studies, you have the ideal opportunity to learn to write English well, and this book can help you achieve that goal.

In addition to accuracy, students on Business and Economics courses are expected to take a critical approach to their sources. This means that your teachers will expect you to question and evaluate everything you read, asking whether it is reliable or relevant. You are also expected to refer carefully to the sources of all your ideas, using a standard system of referencing. *Academic Writing for International Students of Business* will help you to develop these skills.

How is the book organised?

The book can be used either with a teacher or for self-study and reference. Each unit contains practice exercises that can be checked using the answer key at the end of the book. For ease of use, it is divided into the following sections:

Part 1: The Writing Process
This follows the process of writing from the reading stage through to proofreading.

Part 2: Elements of Writing
The key writing skills, organised alphabetically from argument to visual information.

Part 3: Vocabulary for Writing
This section deals with different aspects of academic vocabulary, again arranged alphabetically, from abbreviations to synonyms.

Part 4: Writing Models
Gives examples of the main types of written assignments such as reports, case studies and longer essays.

To help you get the most out of this course, note the following points:

- Instructions are printed as shown here:

  ■ **List your ideas below.**

- Links to relevant units are shown like this:

  ▶ **See Unit 2.13 Style**

  (These links help you to find extra information, but do not have to be read in order to complete the exercises.)

- Answers are provided for most exercises in the answer key at the end of the book. If no definite answer can be given, an example answer is usually offered.

- The **index** can be used to locate specific information. The **glossary** explains academic terms that you may not be familiar with.

Thousands of students have already found that *Academic Writing for International Students of Business* helps them to write more clearly and effectively. This new edition has been developed using their feedback and ideas, and I would be very glad to receive comments and suggestions on any aspect of the book to help develop future editions.

Stephen Bailey
Email: stephen.bailey@w3z.co.uk

Academic Writing Quiz

■ **How much do you know about academic writing? Find out by doing this fun quiz.**

1 The main difference between academic writing and normal writing is that academic writing:
   (a) uses longer words
   (b) tries to be precise and unbiased
   (c) is harder to understand

2 The difference between a project and an essay is:
   (a) essays are longer
   (b) projects are longer
   (c) students choose projects' topics

3 Teachers complain most about students:
   (a) not answering the question given
   (b) not writing enough
   (c) not referencing properly

4 The best time to write an introduction is often:
   (a) first
   (b) last
   (c) after writing the main body

5 Plagiarism is:
   (a) a dangerous disease
   (b) an academic offence
   (c) an academic website

6 Making careful notes is essential for:
   (a) writing essays
   (b) revising for exams
   (c) all academic work

7   An in-text citation looks like:
   (a) (Manton, 2008)
   (b) (Richard Manton, 2008)
   (c) (Manton, R. 2008)

8   Paraphrasing a text means:
   (a) making it shorter
   (b) changing a lot of the vocabulary
   (c) adding more detail

9   Paragraphs always contain:
   (a) six or more sentences
   (b) an example
   (c) a topic sentence

10   The purpose of an introduction is:
   (a) to give your aims and methods
   (b) to excite the reader
   (c) to summarise your ideas

11   Proofreading means:
   (a) getting a friend to check your work
   (b) checking for minor errors
   (c) rewriting

12   Teachers expect students to adopt a critical approach to their sources:
   (a) sometimes
   (b) only for Master's work
   (c) always

Answers on p. 241.

The Writing Process

Background to Writing

Most business schools assess students mainly through written assignments. These include coursework, which may take weeks to write, and exam answers, which often have to be written in an hour or less. This unit deals with:

- the names of different writing tasks
- the format of long and short written texts
- the structure of sentences and paragraphs.

1 The purpose of academic writing

Writers should be clear why they are writing. The most common reasons for writing include:

- to answer a question the writer has been given or chosen
- to report a piece of research the writer has conducted
- to synthesise research done by others on a topic.

■ **Can you suggest any other reasons?**

- _____

- _____

Whatever the purpose, it is helpful to think about the probable readers of your work. How can you explain your ideas to them effectively? Although there is no fixed standard of academic writing, it is clearly different from the written style of newspapers or novels. For example, it is generally agreed that academic writing attempts to be impersonal and objective. What are its other features?

■   Working alone or in a group, list your ideas below.

- _____
- _____
- _____
- _____

2 Common types of academic writing

Below are the most common types of written work produced by business students.

■   Match the terms on the left to the definitions on the right.

Notes	A piece of research, either individual or group work, with the topic chosen by the student(s).
Report	The longest piece of writing normally done by a student (20,000+ words) often for a higher degree, on a topic chosen by the student.
Project	A written record of the main points of a text or lecture, for a student's personal use.
Essay	A general term for any academic essay, report or article.
Dissertation/ Thesis	A study of something that has happened (e.g. a survey a student has conducted).
Paper	The most common type of written work, with the title given by the teacher, normally 1,000–5,000 words.

3 The format of long and short writing tasks

Short essays (including exam answers) generally have this pattern:

Introduction

Main body

Conclusion

Longer essays may include:

Introduction

Main body

      Literature review

      Case study

      Discussion

   References

   Conclusion

   Appendices

▶ **See Unit 4.4 Longer Essays**

Dissertations and journal articles may have:

   Abstract

   List of contents

   List of tables

   Introduction

   Main body

      Literature review

      Case study

      Findings

      Discussion

   Conclusion

   Acknowledgements

   References

   Appendices

■ **Find the words in the lists above that match the following definitions:**

(a) A short summary of 100–200 words that explains the paper's purpose and main findings.

_____

(b) A list of all the sources the writer has mentioned in the text.

_____

(c) A section, at the end, where additional information is included.

_____

(d) A short section where people who have helped the writer are thanked.

_____

(e) Part of the main body in which the views of other writers on the topic are discussed.

_____

(f) A section where one particular example is described in detail.

_____

4 The format of academic writing

There is considerable variation in the format of academic writing required by different business schools and departments. Your teachers may give you guidelines, or you should ask them what they want. But some general features apply to most formats.

■ **Read the text below and identify the features underlined, using the words in the box.**

sentence   heading   sub-title   paragraph   title   phrase

(a) The Effectiveness of Microcredit

(b) An evaluation of programmes in India and the Philippines

(c) Introduction

(d) In the last ten years, considerable claims have been made about the value of microcredit (also known as microfinance), the provision of unsecured small loans to the poor in developing countries. (e) But it has proved surprisingly difficult to accurately measure the effectiveness of these loans, without interference from other non-commercial factors.

(f) Two recent studies have attempted to compare the effects on randomly chosen groups of people with access to microcredit, compared to those without. The first (Bannerjee *et al.*, 2009), based at Massachusetts Institute of Technology (MIT), looked at slumdwellers in the city of Hyderabad in India, while the second (Karlan and Zinman, 2009) compared borrowers and non-borrowers in the Philippines. Overall, neither study found evidence that microcredit had any effect in reducing poverty, although it may have some other positive aspects such as reducing the consumption of alcohol or tobacco.

(a) _____   (d) _____

(b) _____   (e) _____

(c) _____   (f) _____

5 Other common text features

(a) **Reference** to sources: *The first (Bannerjee et al., 2009) looked at slumdwellers . . .*

(b) The use of **abbreviations** to save space: *Massachusetts Institute of Technology (MIT)*

(c) **Italics** used to show words from other languages: Bannerjee *et al.* (= and others)

(d) **Brackets** used to give subsidiary information or to clarify a point: *(also known as microfinance)*

(e) **Numbering systems** (1.1, 1.2) are often used in reports, less so in essays.

6 Simple and longer sentences

■ Study the table below.

Dragon Motors – vehicle production 2009–2013

2009	2010	2011	2012	2013
135,470	156,935	164,820	159,550	123,075

All sentences contain verbs:

> *In 2009, the company produced over 135,000 vehicles.*

> *Between 2009 and 2010, vehicle production increased by 20%.*

Simple sentences (above) are easier to write and read, but longer sentences are also needed in academic writing. However, students should make clarity a priority, and avoid writing very lengthy sentences with several clauses until they feel confident in their ability.

Sentences containing two or more clauses use **conjunctions**, **relative pronouns** or **punctuation** to link the clauses:

> *In 2009, Dragon Motors produced over 135,000 vehicles **but** the following year production increased by 20 per cent.* (conjunction)

> *In 2011, the company built 164,820 vehicles, **which** was the peak of production.* (relative pronoun)

> *Nearly 160,000 vehicles were produced in 2012; by 2013, this had fallen to 123,000.* (punctuation)

■ Write two simple and two longer sentences using data from the table above.

(a) _____

(b) _____

(c) _____

(d) _____

▶ **See Unit 3.6 Numbers**

7 Writing in paragraphs

■ **Discuss the following questions:**

* What is a paragraph?
* Why are texts divided into paragraphs?
* How long are paragraphs?
* Do paragraphs have a standard structure?

■ **Read the text below and divide it into a suitable number of paragraphs.**

INVESTMENT STRATEGIES

Most people want to invest for the future, to cover unexpected financial difficulties and provide security. Different people, however, tend to have different requirements, so that a 25-year-old just leaving university would be investing for long-term capital growth, whereas a 60-year-old who had just retired would probably invest for income. Despite these differences, certain principles apply in most cases. The first issue to consider is risk. In general, the greater the degree of risk, the higher the return. Shares, for example, which can quickly rise or fall in value, typically have a higher yield than bonds, which offer greater stability. Therefore, all investors must decide how much risk is appropriate in their particular situation. Diversification must also be considered in an investment strategy. Wise investors usually seek to spread their investments across a variety of geographical and business sectors. As accurate predictions of the future are almost impossible, it is best to have as many options as possible. A further consideration is investor involvement. Some investors opt for a high degree of involvement and want to buy and sell regularly, constantly watching the markets. But personal involvement can be time-consuming and worrying, and many prefer to leave the management of their portfolios to professional fund managers.

▶ **See Unit 1.9 Organising Paragraphs**

UNIT
1.2

Critical Reading

Students often underestimate the importance of reading effectively, but good reading techniques are vital for success on any business course. This unit:

* examines the most suitable text types for academic work
* explores ways of locating relevant materials in the library
* explains different reading methods
* introduces a critical approach to potential sources.

1 Academic texts

You need to read a variety of text types, such as websites and journal articles, for your course. It is important to identify the most suitable texts and recognise their features, which will help you to assess their value.

■ **You are studying Tourism. Read texts 1–4 on pp. 10–11 and decide which are the most suitable for academic use.**

Text	Suitability?
1	*Yes, it summarises some relevant research and includes citations.*
2	
3	
4	

1

To promote tourism and market destination, it is important to study the tourists' attitude, behaviour and demand. The studies of Levitt (1986) and Kotler and Armstrong (1994) suggest that an understanding of consumer behaviour may help with the marketing planning process in tourism marketing. The research of consumer behaviour is the key to the underpinning of all marketing activity that is carried out to develop, promote and sell tourism products (Swarbrooke and Horner, 1999; Asad, 2005). Therefore, the study of consumer behaviour has become necessary for the sake of tourism marketing.

2

The romance of travel has always fascinated me, and our recent trip to Thailand lived up to expectations. We flew from Gatwick and after a comfortable flight arrived in Bangkok just as the sun was rising. Our stay in the city lasted only a couple of days before we set off for the hill country around Chang Mai, where we were planning to visit some of the indigenous tribes who live in this mountainous region. When we arrived, the weather was rather disappointing, but after a day the heavy rain gave way to sparkling clear sunshine.

3

Holiday trips to the Antarctica have quadrupled in the past decade and last year more than 46,000 people visited the land mass and surrounding oceans. However, safety fears and concerns about the impact visitors are having on the delicate frozen landscape have soared and members of the Antarctic Treaty – an agreement between 28 nations, including the UK, on the use of the continent – are now meeting to discuss ways to regulate tourism.

British officials are seeking to establish a 'strategic agreement for tourism' around the South Pole. If successful, it will see treaty members introduce new measures to improve the safety of tourist trips, while also reducing the impact that visitors will have on the environment. The regulations could see limits on the number of ships and landings, restrictions on how close they come to shore, a ban on building tourist facilities and hotels on the continent, and rules on waste discharges from ships.

4

Equally, from a political perspective, the nature of state involvement in and policies for tourism is dependent on both the political-economic structures and the prevailing political ideology in the destination state, with comparisons typically made between market-led and centrally planned economies. For example, the Thatcher-Reagan-inspired neo-liberalism of the 1980s, and the subsequent focus on privatisation and the markets in many Western nations, contrasted starkly with the then centrally planned tourism sectors in the former Eastern Europe (Buckley and Witt, 1990; Hall, 1991). At the same time, of course, it has also long been recognised that the political-economic relationship of one nation with another or with the wider international community (that is, the extent of political-economic dependency) may represent a significant influence on tourism development (Telfer, 2002). Thus, in short, tourism planning and development in the destination tends to reflect both the structures and political ideologies of the state and its international political-economic relations.

■ **The main features of academic texts are listed in the table below. Find examples of each using the texts above.**

Feature	Example
1 Formal vocabulary	*the marketing planning process in tourism marketing ...* *the extent of political-economic dependency ...*
2 Use of citation	
3 Impersonal style	
4 Long, complex sentences	

2 Types of text

■ The table below lists the most common written sources used by business students. Work with a partner to consider their likely advantages and disadvantages.

Text type	Advantage	Disadvantage
Textbook	*Written for students*	*May be too general or outdated*
Website		
Journal article		
Official report (e.g. from government)		
Newspaper or magazine article		
e-book		

3 Using reading lists

Your teacher may give you a printed reading list, or it may be available online through the library website. The list will usually include textbooks, journal articles and websites. If the list is electronic, there will be links to the library catalogue to let you check on the availability of the material. If the list is printed, you will have to use the library catalogue to find the texts.

You do not have to read every word of a book because it is on the list. Your teacher will probably suggest which pages to read, and also tell you which parts are more important. On reading lists, you will find the following formats:

Books   'The European Workforce: Change and Regulation' (2001) Chapter 6 in S. Mercado, R. Welford and K. Prescott, *European Business*, Fourth Edition, Prentice Hall, London, pp. 203–247

Journal articles W. Mayrhofer and C. Brewster (1996) 'In praise of ethnocentricity: expatriate policies in European multinationals', *The International Executive* 38(6), 749–778

Websites   http://europa.eu/pol/socio/index_en.htm

4 Using library catalogues

University and college libraries usually have online catalogues. These allow students to search for the materials they want in various ways. If the title and author's name are known, it is easy to check if the book is available. But if you are making a search for material on a specific topic, you may have to vary the search terms. For instance, if you want information about exploration for oil, you might try:

- oil exploration
- exploring for oil
- hydrocarbon exploration
- exploring for hydrocarbons

You have been given an essay title: 'Outline the current state of global exploration for oil, and relate this to future levels of production.'

■ **You have entered the term 'oil exploration' in the library catalogue search engine, and these are the seven results. Which would you select to borrow? Give your reasons.**

Full details	Title	Edition/ Year	Location	Holdings
1	Oil exploration and human rights violations in Nigeria's oil producing communities/Olubayo Oloduro.	2013	Main Library	Availability
2	Oil and gas exploration and production (electronic resource): Reserves, costs contracts/Nadine Bret-Rouzaut and Jean-Piere Favennec.	3rd ed. 2011	Main Library	Availability
3	Deepwater pretroleum exploration & production [electronic resource]: a nontechnical guide William L. Leffler, Richard Pattarozzi, Gordon Sterling.	2011	Main Library	Availability
4	Hydrocarbon exploration and production/by Frank Jahn, Mark Cook and Mark Graham.	2nd ed. 2008	Science Library	Availability
5	China and the global energy crisis: development and prospects for China's oil and natural gas/Tatsu Kambara, Christopher Howe.	2007	Main Library	Availability

Full details	Title	Edition/ Year	Location	Holdings
<u>6</u>	Operational aspects of oil and gas well testing [electronic resource]/Stuart McAleese.	2000	Main Library	<u>Availability</u>
<u>7</u>	Geophysical exploration: an outline of the principal methods used in the search for minerals, oil, gas and water supplies/F.W. Dunning.	1970	Science Library	<u>Availability</u>

Full details
If you click on this, you will get more information about the book, including the number of pages and a summary of the contents. If a book has more than one edition, it suggests that it is a successful title. This may help you decide whether to borrow it.

Year
The most recent books are listed first; always try to use the most up-to-date sources.

Location
Many large universities have more than one library. This tells you which one the book is kept in.

Holdings
If you click on availability, it will tell you how many copies the library holds and if they are available to borrow or out on loan.

5 Using library websites to search journals and electronic resources

Journals are specialised academic publications produced on a regular basis, containing recent research. You need to be familiar with the main journals in your subject area. They are usually available in paper or electronic formats (e-journals).

E-journals and other electronic resources such as subject databases are becoming increasingly important. Their advantage is that they can be accessed by computer, saving the need to visit the library to find a book. Most library websites have a separate portal or gateway for searching electronic resources. This allows you to enter the name of a specific journal, or look for possible journals in your subject area by entering a term such as 'international business law'. In this case, the database may offer the following titles:

- *European Business Law Review*
- *European Business Organisation Law Review*
- *International Trade and Business Law Review*
- *Law and Business Review of the Americas*

In each case, you can access a list of issues available. In the case of *European Business Organisation Law Review*, the list would include:

- Dec 2013 Vol. 14 Issue 4
- Sep 2013 Vol. 14 Issue 3
- June 2013 Vol. 14 Issue 2
- Mar 2013 Vol. 14 Issue 1

By clicking on any of these issues, you can read a full list of articles. It is usually sufficient to read the abstract to find out if the article will be relevant to your work. Note that most journal websites contain a search engine to allow you to search all back issues by subject. They may also offer links to articles in other journals on the same topic.

The best way to become familiar with these methods is to practise. Library websites usually contain tutorials for new students, and librarians are always willing to give help and advice when needed.

■ **Select a specific topic from your subject area.**

(a) Use the library catalogue to search for relevant books. Write down the most useful titles.

(b) Look for a few relevant journal articles, using the library portal. Write a reference for each article.

6 Reading methods

It is easy for students to underestimate the importance of reading skills. Especially for international students, reading academic texts in the quantity required for most courses is a demanding task. But students will not benefit from attending lectures and seminars unless the reading is done promptly, while clearly most writing tasks require extensive reading.

Moreover, the texts often contain new vocabulary and phrases, and may be written in a rather formal style. Clearly, you do not have time to read every word published on the topic you are studying. This means that distinct methods have to be adopted to cope with the volume of reading required, which is especially important when you are reading in another language. The chart on p. 16 illustrates an approach to finding and dealing with texts.

■ **Complete the empty boxes in the chart with the following techniques:**

- Read intensively to make notes on key points.
- Scan text for information you need (e.g. names).
- Survey text features (e.g. abstract, contents, index).

Choosing suitable texts

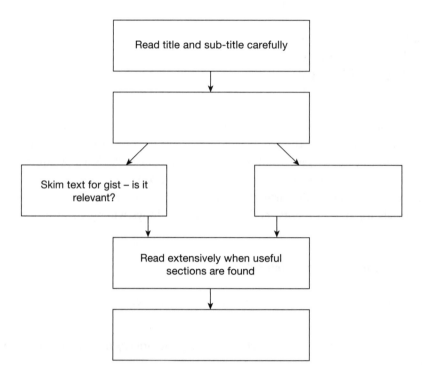

Read title and sub-title carefully

Skim text for gist – is it relevant?

Read extensively when useful sections are found

■ **Answer the following questions:**

(a) What is the difference between skimming and scanning?

(b) Can you suggest any other reading skills to add to the chart above?

7 Titles, subtitles and text features

Many books and articles have both a title and a subtitle:

> *Much Ado about Nothing? Do domestic firms really benefit from foreign direct investment?*

The title is usually shorter; the subtitle often gives more information about the focus.

After finding a relevant text, it is worth checking the following text features before starting to read:

Author
Is the writer well known in his/her field? What else has he/she published?

Publication date and edition
Do not use a first edition if there is a (revised) second edition available.

Abstract

All journal articles have an abstract, which is a paragraph summarising the purpose and conclusions of the article. Reading this should give you a good idea of the relevance of the text for you.

Contents

A list of the main chapters or sections. This should tell you how much space is devoted to the topic you are researching.

Introduction or preface

This is where the author often explains the aim or purpose of the paper, and also how the text is organised.

References

This list shows all the sources used by the author and referred to in the text. It may give you some suggestions for further reading. (In the USA, this is usually called the bibliography.)

Index

An alphabetical list of all the topics and names mentioned in a book. If, for example, you are looking for information about a person, the index will tell you if that person is mentioned, and how often.

8 Assessing texts critically

You cannot afford to waste time on texts that are unreliable or out of date. If you are using material that is not on the reading list, you must assess it critically to ensure that the writer can be trusted and the material is trustworthy.

■ Compare these two texts on a pharmaceutical company. Which is the more reliable?

1

Our success is based on a commitment to discovery, finding new ideas that are inspired by life and which in turn help to inspire the lives of our stakeholders. We discover new medicines that are designed to improve the health and quality of life of patients around the world – medicines which are innovative, effective and which offer added benefits such as reduced side effects or better ways of taking the treatment. We also focus on getting the best from every medicine we make by exploring all the ways it can be used or improved. With a global business comes a global responsibility for consistently high standards of behaviour worldwide. We aim to effectively manage that responsibility and help to find new ways of bringing benefit to society to ensure that Medmax continues to be welcomed as a valued member of the global community.

2

Recent trading results from Medmax show an apparently healthy position, with pre-tax profit rising by 24% and total revenues up 5%. These figures, however, were inflated by some one-off gains, such as a $152 million sale of swine flu vaccine to the US government. Sales of the ZX high blood pressure drug also increased sharply due to its main rival being temporarily off the market due to safety concerns. Costs were very significantly lower in the last quarter, falling 14%, due to productivity improvements. The anti-cholesterol drug Somar also sold very well, becoming the market leader, but there are concerns that a pending US court case may soon challenge Medmax's patent on this product. There are also worries that re-organisation of the American healthcare system may affect Medmax's long-term profits, and the company's shares have recently fallen by 6%.

The first text contains little or no precise information about the company's performance and is full of statements that cannot be checked (medicines that are innovative, effective . . .). It appears to be taken from the company website. By contrast, the second seems to be based on a recent financial report and contains both facts (profits rising by 24%) and some comment (may affect Medmax's long-term profits). The first text is of little use to a student, but the second could be used, with care, for analysis of the company's current state.

■ **Read the following texts and decide if they are reliable or not. Give reasons for your decisions in the table opposite.**

1

Hard up? Why struggle when you could live in luxury? Solve your money worries easily and quickly by working for us. No experience needed, you can earn hundreds of pounds for just a few hours' work per day. Work when it suits you, day or night. Don't delay, call today for an interview on 07795-246791.

2

If you have money problems, there's lots of ways you can save cash. Instead of spending money on new clothes, try buying them secondhand from charity shops, where you'll find lots of stylish bargains. Eating out is another big expense, but instead you can get together with a few friends and cook a meal together; it's cheaper and it's fun. Bus fares and taxis can also cost a lot, so it might be worth looking for a cheap bicycle, which lets you travel where you want, when you want.

3

Most students find that they have financial difficulties at times. It has been estimated that nearly 55% experience financial difficulties in their first year at college or university. It's often hard living on a small fixed income, and the cost of accommodation and food can come as a shock when you first live away from your parents. The most important thing, if you find you are getting into debt, is to speak to a financial advisor in the Student Union, who may be able to help you sort out your problems.

1	
2	
3	

■   You are writing an essay on diversification in business. You find the following article in a recent magazine. Read it critically and decide whether you could use it in your work.

CHANGE ON THE FARM

In the last 20 years the structure of British farming has changed significantly. Many small farms have been merged to create fewer mega-farms, with all the benefits of scale. But another important development has been to increase the income obtained from activities other than growing food. In Earlswood, Warwickshire a farmer has created a three-hectare 'maize maze' which over 15,000 people have paid £5 to explore during the summer. This more than compensates for the cost of designing and cutting the attraction. In the autumn, over 80% of the maize should still be saleable as cattle feed, giving the farmer a double income. Such enterprises are examples of the new 'agritainment' sector, along with bed-and-breakfast accommodation, shooting ranges and wedding venues.

The Department for the Environment, Food and Rural Affairs (DEFRA) estimates that over 10% of farms have diversified their income by offering recreational activities, and over 15% of farm income is now derived from such sources. This has provided farmers with a cushion against the swings of commodity prices in the last few years, although with the current rise in global food prices farmers may be becoming less interested in converting their old barns into craft workshops.

Positive aspects: _____

Negative aspects: _____

9 Critical thinking

Even when you feel that a text is reliable and that you can safely use it as a source, it is still important to adopt a critical attitude towards it. This approach is perhaps easiest to learn when reading, but is important for all other academic work (i.e. listening, discussing and writing). Critical thinking means not just passively accepting what you hear or read, but instead actively questioning and assessing it. As you read, you should ask yourself the following questions:

(a) What are the key ideas in this?
(b) Does the thesis of the writer develop logically, step by step?
(c) Are the examples given helpful? Would other examples be better?
(d) Does the author have any bias (leaning to one side or the other)?

(e) Does the evidence presented seem reliable, in my experience?

(f) Do I agree with the writer's views?

■   **Read critically the two articles on universities.**

A. COLLEGE CONCERNS

Despite their dominance of global league tables (e.g. Shanghai Rankings Consultancy) American universities currently face significant criticism. The American Enterprise Institute (AEI) and the Goldwater Institute have recently published negative reports on US universities, while a highly critical book (Hacker and Dreifus) was published in 2010. The critics focus on the rising costs of American higher education, which have increased at a much faster rate than inflation, resulting in a situation where even middle-class families are finding the expense unsupportable.

Another target of criticism is the focus on research at the expense of teaching. Students rarely meet the 'star' professors, being taught instead by badly-paid graduate students. It is claimed that in one year nearly half of Harvard's history professors were on sabbatical leave. As a consequence, students work less; according to the AEI they currently study for 14 hours per week, whereas 50 years ago the figure was 24 hours per week. Despite this the proportion of students gaining a first or 2.1 degree has increased significantly: a situation described by the critics as 'grade inflation'.

B. A BRIGHTER TOMORROW?

There is little doubt that a university degree is the key to a better future for any student. Despite the costs involved in terms of fees, it has been calculated that the average UK university graduate will earn £400,000 ($600,000) more over his or her lifetime compared to a non-graduate. Possession of a degree should also assist a graduate find a satisfying job more quickly and give greater prospects for promotion inside the chosen career. A degree from a British university is recognised all over the world as proof of a high quality education.

A university course will not only provide students with up-to-date knowledge in their subject area, but also provide practice with the essential skills required by many employers today, such as the ability to communicate effectively using ICT, or the skills of team working and problem solving. In addition, living away from home in an international atmosphere gives the opportunity to make new friends from all over the world, and build networks of contacts that may be invaluable in a future career.

Studying at university is a unique opportunity for many young people to develop individually by acquiring independence, free from parental control. They will learn to look after themselves in a secure environment, and gain useful life skills such as cooking and budgeting. Most graduates look back at their degree courses as a valuable experience at a critical period of their lives.

■ List any statements from the articles that you find unreliable, and add comments to explain your doubts in the table below. Then decide which article you find more reliable overall.

Statements	Comments
A	
B	

▶ See Unit 2.1 Argument and Discussion

10 Vocabulary revision

■ Match the nouns on the left, which have all occurred in this unit, with their definitions on the right.

Stakeholders	Employees of an organisation
Productivity	Preference for one point of view
Patent	Money owed
Debt	Process of selling state-owned assets
Commodity prices	A measure of a company's output per worker
Workforce	All parties involved in a business
Budgeting	Cost of raw materials such as wheat or oil
Privatisation	Spreading business activities over several areas
Bias	Process of planning future spending priorities
Diversification	Method of protecting new inventions from copying

Avoiding Plagiarism

Plagiarism is a concern both for teachers and students, but it can be avoided by understanding the issues involved. In the English-speaking academic world, it is essential to use a wide range of sources for your writing and to acknowledge these sources clearly. This unit introduces the techniques students need to do this. Further practice is provided in Units 1.6 Summarising and Paraphrasing and 1.7 References and Quotations.

1 What is plagiarism?

Basically, plagiarism means taking ideas or words from a source (e.g. a book or journal) without giving credit (acknowledgement) to the author. In academic work, ideas and words are seen as private property belonging to the person who first thought or wrote them. If you borrow or refer to the work of another person, you must show that you have done this by providing the correct acknowledgement. This is done by the following methods:

Summary and citation

> *Rodgers (2007) argues that family-owned businesses survive recessions better.*

Quotation and citation

> *As Rodgers maintains: 'There is strong evidence for the resilience of family businesses in recessionary times' (Rodgers, 2007: 23).*

These citations are linked to a list of **references** at the end of the main text, which include the following details:

Author	Date	Title	Place of publication	Publisher
Rodgers, F.	(2007)	*The Family Business: A re-assessment*	Oxford	Critchlow

This reference gives the reader the necessary information to find the source if more detail is required. The citations make it clear to the reader that you have read Rodgers and borrowed this idea from him. Not to do this is seen as a kind of theft, and as such is considered to be an academic crime. Therefore, it is important for all students, including international ones, to understand the meaning of plagiarism and learn how to prevent it in their work.

▶ **See Unit 1.7 References and Quotations**

2 Degrees of plagiarism

Although plagiarism essentially means copying somebody else's work, it is not always easy to define.

■ Working with a partner, consider the following academic situations and decide if they are plagiarism.

	Situation	Plagiarism? Yes/No
1	Copying a paragraph, but changing a few words and giving a citation.	
2	Cutting and pasting a short article from a website, with no citation.	
3	Taking two paragraphs from a classmate's essay, without citation.	
4	Taking a graph from a textbook, giving the source.	
5	Taking a quotation from a source, giving a citation but not using quotation marks.	
6	Using an idea that you think of as general knowledge (e.g. the Great Depression was caused by restrictions on free trade), without citation.	
7	Using a paragraph from an essay you wrote and had marked the previous semester, without citation.	
8	Using the results of your own research (e.g. from a survey), without citation.	
9	Discussing an essay topic with a group of classmates and using some of their ideas in your own work.	
10	Giving a citation for some information but misspelling the author's name.	

Students who plagiarise often do so accidentally. For example, situation 10 on p. 25, when the author's name is misspelt, is technically plagiarism but really carelessness. In situation 9, your teacher may have encouraged you to discuss the topic in groups, and then write an essay on your own, in which case it would not be plagiarism. Self-plagiarism is also possible, as in situation 7. It can be difficult to decide what is general or common knowledge (situation 6), but you can always try asking colleagues.

However, it is not a good excuse to say that you didn't know the rules of plagiarism, or that you didn't have time to write in your own words. Nor is it adequate to say that the rules are different in your own country. In general, anything that is not common knowledge or your own ideas and research (published or not) must be cited and referenced.

3 Avoiding plagiarism by summarising and paraphrasing

Quotations should not be overused, so you must learn to paraphrase and summarise in order to include other writers' ideas in your work.

- Paraphrasing involves rewriting a text so that the language is substantially different while the content stays the same.
- Summarising means reducing the length of a text but retaining the main points.

Normally, both skills are used at the same time, as can be seen in the examples below.

▶ **See Unit 1.6 Summarising and Paraphrasing**

■ **Read the following text and then compare the five paragraphs opposite, which use ideas and information from it. Decide which are plagiarised and which are acceptable, and give your reasons in the table opposite.**

RAILWAY MANIAS

In 1830 there were a few dozen miles of railways in all the world – chiefly consisting of the line from Liverpool to Manchester. By 1840 there were over 4,500 miles, by 1850 over 23,500. Most of them were projected in a few bursts of speculative frenzy known as the 'railway manias' of 1835–1837 and especially in 1844–1847; most of them were built in large part with British capital, British iron, machines and know-how. These investment booms appear irrational, because in fact few railways were much more profitable to the investor than other forms of enterprise, most yielded quite modest profits and many none at all: in 1855 the average interest on capital sunk in the British railways was a mere 3.7%.

(From *The Age of Revolution* by Eric Hobsbawm, 1995, p. 45)

(a) Between 1830 and 1850, there was very rapid development in railway construction worldwide. Two periods of especially feverish growth were 1835–1837 and 1844–1847. It is hard to understand the reason for this intense activity, since railways were not particularly profitable investments and some produced no return at all (Hobsbawm, 1995: 45).

(b) There were only a few dozen miles of railways in 1830, including the Liverpool to Manchester line. But by 1840, there were over 4,500 miles and over 23,500 by 1850. Most of them were built in large part with British capital, British iron, machines and know-how, and most of them were projected in a few bursts of speculative frenzy known as the 'railway manias' of 1835–1837 and especially in 1844–1847. Because most yielded quite modest profits, and many none at all, these investment booms appear irrational. In fact, few railways were much more profitable to the investor than other forms of enterprise (Hobsbawm, 1995: 45).

(c) As Hobsbawm (1995) argues, nineteenth-century railway mania was partly irrational: 'because in fact few railways were much more profitable to the investor than other forms of enterprise, most yielded quite modest profits and many none at all: in 1855 the average interest on capital sunk in the British railways was a mere 3.7%' (Hobsbawm, 1995: 45).

(d) Globally, railway networks increased dramatically from 1830 to 1850, the majority in short periods of 'mania' (1835–1837 and 1844–1847). British technology and capital were responsible for much of this growth, yet the returns on the investment were hardly any better than comparable business opportunities (Hobsbawm, 1895: 45).

(e) The dramatic growth of railways between 1830 and 1850 was largely achieved using British technology. However, it has been claimed that much of this development was irrational because few railways were much more profitable to the investor than other forms of enterprise; most yielded quite modest profits and many none at all.

	Plagiarised or acceptable?
(a)	
(b)	
(c)	
(d)	
(e)	

4 Avoiding plagiarism by developing good study habits

Few students deliberately try to cheat by plagiarising, but some develop poor study habits that result in the risk of plagiarism.

■ **Working with a partner, add to the list of positive habits.**

- Plan your work carefully so you don't have to write the essay at the last minute.

- Take care to make notes in your own words, not copying from the source.

- Keep a record of all the sources you use (e.g. author, date, title, page numbers, publisher).

- Make sure all your in-text citations are included in the list of references.

5 Vocabulary revision

■ **Revise this unit by matching the words on the left with the definitions on the right.**

Source	Using the exact words of the original text in your work
Citation	To gain advantage dishonestly
To summarise	Short in-text note giving the author's name and publication date
Quotation	To reduce the length of a text but keeping the main points
Reference	Any text that students use to obtain ideas or information
To cheat	Full publication details of a text to allow a reader to access the original

6 Research

Does your college or university have a policy on plagiarism? Look on the website to find out. It may raise some issues that you want to discuss with colleagues or your teachers.

If you can't find anything for your institution, try one of these sites:

http://owl.english.purdue.edu/owl/resource/589/01/
www.uefap.com/writing/plagiar/plagfram.htm

From Understanding Titles to Planning

In both exams and coursework, it is essential for students to understand what an essay title is asking them to do. A plan can then be drawn up, which should prevent time being wasted, while ensuring the question is answered fully. This unit looks at:

- key words in titles
- essay length and organisation
- alternative methods of essay planning.

1 The planning process

Teachers frequently complain that students do not answer the question set, but this can be avoided by care at the planning stage. Planning is necessary in all academic writing, but clearly there are important differences between planning in exams, when time is short, and for coursework, when preparatory reading is required. However, in both cases, the process of planning should include these three steps:

1 Analyse the title wording
2 Decide how long each section should be
3 Prepare an outline using your favourite method

▶ **See Unit 4.4 Longer Essays**

2 Analysing essay titles

Titles contain key words that tell the student what to do. Note that titles often have two (or more) parts:

> **What** *is meant by a demand curve and* **why** *would we expect it to slope downwards?*

In this case, 'what' is asking for a description and 'why' for a reason or explanation.

■ Underline the key words in the following titles and consider what they are asking you to do.

(a) Summarise the main reasons for the growth of e-commerce, and discuss the likely results of this.

(b) 'The internet has rendered obsolete the traditional theories of the internationalisation of firms.' Critically evaluate this statement.

(c) Describe the barriers and challenges to managing diversity and critically examine organisational practices.

(d) Discuss the relationship between knowledge and power in organisations. Consider the implications for managers.

3 Practice: key words

■ Match the key words on the left to the definitions on the right.

Analyse	Explain a topic briefly and clearly
Assess/Evaluate	Deal with a complex subject by reducing it to the main elements
Describe	Divide into sections and discuss each critically/consider widely
Discuss	Break down into the various parts and their relationships
Examine/Explore	Make a proposal and support it
Illustrate	Look at various aspects of a topic, compare benefits and drawbacks
Outline/Trace	Give a detailed account of something
Suggest	Give examples
Summarise	Decide the value or worth of a subject

4 Brainstorming

It is often helpful to start thinking about a topic by writing down the ideas you have, in any order. Taking the example from 2(a) opposite, you might collect the following points:

<u>Growth of e-commerce – likely results</u>

Main reasons

- businesses can offer a wider range of products via internet
- more convenient for customers than travelling to shops
- businesses can reduce overheads by centralising distribution centres
- prices can often be lower.

Likely results

- decline in conventional shops
- growth in delivery businesses
- shopping centres become entertainment areas.

■ **Working with a partner, brainstorm ideas for the title below:**

> How and why has the market for international tourism segmented since the middle of the twentieth century? What are the economic forces that have driven this process?

5 Essay length

Coursework essays usually have a required length, normally between 1,000 and 5,000 words. You must keep to this limit, although deviations of 5% more or less are generally acceptable. However, at the planning stage, you need to consider what proportion of the essay to allocate to each part of the question.

As a basic guide, 20% is usually sufficient for the introduction and conclusion together (references are not included in the word count). Therefore, in a 2,000-word essay, the main body would have 1,600 words.

If this was the length given for title 2(a) pn p. 30, you might decide on the following division for the main body:

Reasons that benefit businesses: reduced overheads/wider range	600 words
Reasons that benefit customers: convenience and lower prices	450 words
Likely results: fewer shops/change in use/more deliveries	550 words
Total	**1,600 words**

This calculation is useful since it can guide the amount of reading you need to do, as well as providing the basis for an outline. Moreover, it prevents you from writing an unbalanced answer, in which part of the question is not fully developed.

Essays in exams do not have a word limit, but it is equally important to plan them in similar terms (e.g. part 1, 40%, part 2, 60%).

■   **Identify the key words in the following titles and decide what percentage of the main body to give to each part.**

Title	Part 1 (%)	Part 2 (%)
(a) Describe the typical social, cultural and environmental impacts experienced by tourist destinations in developing countries. How can harmful impacts be reduced or avoided?		
(b) 'Monopolies are inefficient in using resources.' Explain and discuss.		
(c) What problems do East Asian businesses face in integrating with the global economy? Discuss with reference to a country example.		

6 Outlines

An outline should help the writer to answer the question as effectively as possible. Care at this stage will save wasted effort later. The more detail you include in your outline, the easier the writing process will be.

Note that for coursework, it is usually better to write the main body first, then the introduction and finally the conclusion. Therefore, you may prefer to outline just the main body at this stage.

There is no fixed pattern for an outline; different methods appeal to different students.

For example, with the first part of title 2(a) above:

'Summarise the main reasons for the growth of e-commerce'

(a) The outline might be a list:

1   Benefits for buyers
   - greater convenience in shopping by computer at any time
   - lower prices
   - better choice.

2   Benefits for sellers
   - cost saving by centralising distribution
   - global customer base
   - 24/7 trading.

(b) An alternative is a mind map:

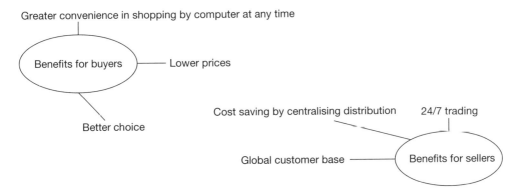

■ **(c) Discuss the advantages and drawbacks of each method with a partner.**

■ **(d) Prepare an outline for the second part of the same title, using either method:**

'Discuss the likely results of this.'

Finding Key Points and Note-making

After finding a suitable source and identifying relevant sections of text, the next step is to select the key points that relate to your topic and make notes on them. This unit explains and practises this process, which also involves skills developed in Unit 1.6 Summarising and Paraphrasing.

1 Finding key points

Before making notes, you need to find the main ideas in a text. These are included in the topic sentence, which is often, but not always, the first sentence of a paragraph.

■ Read the following paragraph, about the growing market for products designed for older people, and underline two key points. Then choose a title for the paragraph.

Title: _____

The generation born after World War II, sometimes called the baby-boomers, are now reaching retirement age, and businesses are starting to realise that they are a wealthier market than any previous retirement group. Financial products, travel and medicines are well-established industries which interest the over-60s, but others are now focusing on this age group. Volkswagen, for instance, has produced a car with raised seats and more interior space to appeal to their tastes. In Japan, with its ageing population, companies have more experience of selling to the retired and have been successful with unusual products such as a robotic seal, which serves as a pet substitute for the lonely. There are, however, certain difficulties in selling to this market. Some customers resent being addressed as 'old' since they see themselves as more youthful, while there is a huge variation in the profile of the baby boomers, ranging from healthy and active to the bed-ridden and infirm.

2 Finding relevant points

When preparing to write an essay, you have to search for information and ideas relevant to your subject. Therefore, the key points that you select must relate to that topic.

You are given an essay title: 'Taxation as an instrument of social policy – discuss.'

■ **Read the following article and underline the key points that relate to your essay topic.**

CAN TAXATION REDUCE OBESITY?

Taxation has been imposed by governments for thousands of years, and initially the basis of taxation was something easily assessed, such as land, hearths or windows, all of which were difficult to hide from the tax collector. But in more recent times governments have sought to use taxes not just to raise revenue, but also to reward virtue and discourage vice.

The practice of imposing taxes on products which are thought to have a negative social impact, such as alcohol, has been accepted for several hundred years, and are now called Pigouvian taxes (after the twentieth-century economist Arthur Pigou). Tobacco, gambling and carbon taxes are common examples. It has recently been suggested in the USA that so-called junk food should be taxed in order to compensate for the social costs of the obesity it is believed to cause. This proposal is based on the estimate of the medical costs of obesity, which is thought to be linked to cancer, diabetes and heart disease. These costs are shared by all taxpayers, not just the obese, so it is claimed that taxing items such as hamburgers and sugary drinks would both reduce consumption and help pay for medical care.

A study of the long-term effects of changes in food prices (Goldman, Lakdawalla and Zheng, 2009) argues that significant changes in consumption, and hence obesity levels, can be achieved over the long-term. They claim that raising the price of calories by 10% could eliminate nearly half the increase in obesity over a 20-year span. But the link between junk food and ill-health is not easily determined. A physically active person could eat hamburgers daily and still keep slim. In this respect it is quite different from drinking alcohol or causing air pollution.

It has even been suggested that such a 'fat tax' might have the opposite effect and reduce activity levels by forcing people to spend more time preparing food for themselves, instead of buying it from fast-food outlets (Yaniv, Rosin and Tobol, 2009). Additionally, other studies on the effects of alcohol and tobacco taxes indicate that the heaviest users of these products are the least influenced by price rises, so that raising the price of hamburgers may do little to curb consumption among the most avid consumers. As these are often also the poorest, the tax would not only fail to improve their health, but would be regressive, making them even poorer.

(Rohan, J. (2010) *Public Health Review* 8, p. 36)

3 Practice A

■   Complete the set of notes for 'Can taxation reduce obesity?' using the key points underlined above.

Source: Rohan, J. (2010) *Public Health Review* 8, p. 36

<u>Taxing junk food</u>

(1) *Goods > social harm (e.g. alcohol) have been taxed since 18th C.*

(2) *US proposal to tax junk food > reduce obesity > cut medical costs (diabetes, heart disease)*

(3) _____

_____

(4) _____

_____

(5) _____

_____

(6) _____

_____

4 Why make notes?

■   What are the main reasons for note-making? Add to the list below.

(a)   *To prepare for essay writing*

(b)   _____

(c)   _____

(d)   _____

(e)   _____

5 Note-making methods

■   You are looking for information on the current media revolution. Study the text below (key points underlined) and the notes in the box. What do you notice about the language of the notes?

THE DEATH OF THE PRESS?

A hundred years ago news was exclusively provided by newspapers. There was no other way of supplying the latest information on politics, crime, finance or sport to the millions of people who bought and read newspapers, sometimes twice a day. Today the situation is very different. The same news is also available on television, radio and the internet, and because of the nature of these media, can be more up-to-date than in print. For young people, especially, the internet has become the natural source of news and comment.

This development means that in many countries newspaper circulation is falling, and a loss of readers also means a fall in advertising, which is the main income for most papers. Consequently, in both Britain and the USA newspapers are closing every week. But when a local newspaper goes out of business an important part of the community is lost. It allows debate on local issues, as well as providing a noticeboard for events such as weddings and society meetings.

All newspapers are concerned by these developments, and many have tried to find methods of increasing their sales. One approach is to focus on magazine-type articles rather than news, another is to give free gifts such as DVDs, while others have developed their own websites to provide continuous news coverage. However, as so much is now freely available online to anyone with a web browser, none of these have had a significant impact on the steady decline of paid-for newspapers.

Source: *New Business Monthly*, May 2010, p. 37

Decline of Newspapers   (*New Business Monthly*, May 2010, p. 37)

(a) Newspapers only source of news 100 yrs ago – now also TV, radio + www

(b) Newspaper sales > decline in advertising > newspapers shutting

(c) Attempts to increase sales: •   more magazine content

                                        •   gifts

                                        •   websites

(d) but none very effective

6 Effective note-making

Notes are for your personal use and you should create your own style.

(a) You must use your own words and not copy phrases from the original to avoid the risk of plagiarism. The quantity of notes you make depends on your task: you may only need a few points, or a lot of detail.

(b) Always record the source of your notes, to save time when you have to write the list of references.

(c) Notes are written quickly, so keep them simple. Do not write sentences. Leave out articles (a/the) and prepositions (of/to).

(d) If you write lists, it is important to have clear headings (underlined) and numbering systems (a, b, c, or 1, 2, 3) to organise the information. Do not crowd your notes.

(e) Use symbols (+, >, =) to save time.

(f) Use abbreviations (e.g. = for example). You need to make up your own abbreviations for your subject area. But do not abbreviate too much, or you may find your notes hard to understand in the future!

▶   See Unit 3.2 Abbreviations

7 Practice B

You have to write an essay titled: 'What is the value of anti-monopoly legislation?'

■   **Read the following text, underline the relevant key points and make notes on them.**

THE DIFFICULTY OF ASSESSING PREDATORY PRICING

Small companies often feel that larger rivals want to put them out of business by discounting, for example the corner shop which cannot match the supermarket's bargain offers. In 1890 the United States passed the Sherman Antitrust Act, which was an attempt to prevent large companies exploiting their semi-monopoly position, and many countries have adopted similar legislation. This is a response to concerns that big businesses will lower prices to drive competitors to bankruptcy, and then be able to raise prices at will.

But clearly low prices are an advantage to consumers, and proving predation in court is a difficult process. Firms may have legitimate reasons for selling below cost, such as promoting a new product or because they expect their costs to fall when volume increases. In these cases current losses can be offset against future profits. Bundling goods, i.e. selling two or more products as a package, makes it even harder to establish malpractice. This is because the profit margin on each item in the bundle may vary. So a company that makes little profit on printers may sell them with higher profit margin ink cartridges. By doing this it can claim that other costs are being saved, for example on distribution.

In May 2009 the European Union found the chip-maker Intel guilty of predatory pricing against a rival, AMD, and fined the company 1.06 billion euros, claiming that European consumers of computers had suffered as a result of Intel providing incentives to manufacturers to favour its chips. But Intel appealed against the verdict, and the complexity of the case (the court verdict ran to over 500 pages) is an example of the difficulty of policing companies in this area.

(Caballero J. and Poledna Z. (2010) *European Business Prospects*, London: University Press, p. 351)

8 Vocabulary revision

■ Explain the following phrases from this unit to a partner.

(a) financial products

(b) negative social impact

(c) curb consumption

(d) regressive taxation

(e) anti-monopoly legislation

(f) predatory pricing

(g) drive competitors to bankruptcy

(h) losses can be offset

(i) establish malpractice

(j) newspaper circulation

Summarising and Paraphrasing

Summarising and paraphrasing are normally used together in academic writing. Summarising allows the writer to condense lengthy sources into a concise form, while paraphrasing means changing the wording of a text so that it is significantly different from the original source, without changing the meaning. Both are needed to avoid the risk of plagiarism, and this unit practises them separately and jointly.

1 What makes a good summary?

■ Write a summary of one of the topics below in no more than 20 words.

(a) A company you have worked for

(b) A town or city you know well

(c) A product you have recently bought

_____

_____

_____

■ Compare your summary with others in your group. What is needed for a good summary?

• _____

• _____

• _____

2 Stages of summarising

Summarising is a flexible tool. You can use it to give a one-sentence outline of an article, or to provide much more detail, depending on your needs. Generally, a summary focuses on the main ideas and excludes examples or supporting information. In every case, the same basic steps need to be followed in order to meet the criteria discussed in section 1 on p. 41.

■ **Study the stages of summary writing below, which have been mixed up. Put them in the correct order (1–5).**

(a) Write the summary from your notes, reorganising the structure if needed.

(b) Make notes of the key points, paraphrasing where possible.

(c) Read the original text carefully and check any new or difficult vocabulary.

(d) Mark the key points by underlining or highlighting.

(e) Check the summary to ensure it is accurate and nothing important has been changed or lost.

3 Practice A

■ **Read the following text and the summaries that follow. Rate them from 1 (best) to 3.**

DISRUPTIVE TECHNOLOGY

This phrase was first used by Joseph Bower and Clayton Christensen, of the Harvard Business School, in 1995. They employed it to describe a new technology that appeals to a minority section of the market, but a large enough minority to allow the technology to take root and develop. Companies that continue to use the older technology run the risk of being left behind if they do not adopt the innovation at the right moment. A clear example in the mid-1990s was the digital camera. The first models had lower picture quality than film cameras and were expensive. But their important advantages were the ability of the photographer to see the results immediately, and being able to download the images to a computer for storage, printing or emailing. Since then, digital cameras have completely transformed the industry. The business of making film has almost vanished, and the vast majority of cameras sold are now digital.

(a) Disruptive technology, according to two researchers from the Harvard Business School, is a new invention that attracts enough buyers to become established in the market, and then to improve and grow. For example, the first digital cameras, launched in the mid-1990s, took poor quality pictures and were costly, but had some important benefits. Today, they dominate the market, and the older type of camera that uses film is now less popular.

(b) Bower and Christensen introduced the term 'disruptive technology' in 1995, to characterise a new technology that sold well enough to enter the market, and could then be developed further. The digital camera, for instance, was originally expensive and had low picture quality. However, it had certain advantages that quickly allowed it to virtually replace traditional film cameras.

(c) Digital cameras are a good example of a disruptive technology, a term used by Bower and Christensen of Harvard Business School in 1995 to describe a new technology that initially wins enough market share to survive and develop. These cameras at first produced inferior pictures, but had the advantages of showing the photo instantly, and allowing the user to download the image. In a few years, they became dominant in the camera market, while traditional film cameras were almost redundant.

4 Practice B

■ (a) Read the following text and underline the key points.

WEALTH AND FERTILITY

For most of the past century, an inverse correlation between human fertility and economic development has been found. This means that as a country got richer, the average number of children born to each woman got smaller. While in the poorest countries women often have eight children, the rate fell as low as 1.3 in some European countries such as Italy, which is below the replacement rate. Such a low rate has two likely negative consequences: the population will fall in the long-term, and a growing number of old people will have to be supported by a shrinking number of young. But a recent study by researchers from Pennsylvania University suggests that this pattern may be changing. They related countries' fertility rates to their human development index (HDI), a figure with a maximum value of 1.0, which assesses life expectancy, average income and education level. Over 20 countries now have an HDI of more than 0.9, and in a majority of these the fertility rate has started to increase, and in some is approaching two children per woman. Although there are exceptions such as Japan, it appears that ever higher levels of wealth and education eventually translate into a desire for more children.

▶   **See Unit 1.5 Finding Key Points and Note-making**

■   **(b) Complete the notes of the key points below.**

(i)   Falling levels of fertility have generally been found _____.

(ii)   In some, number of children born _____.

(iii) Two results: smaller populations and _____.

(iv)   Recent research claims that _____.

(v)   Comparison of HDI (human development index: _____)
       with fertility found that in most highly rated (+0.9) countries,
       _____.

■   **(c) Join the notes together and expand them to make the final summary. Check that the meaning is clear and no important points have been left out. Find a suitable title.**

Title: _____

This summary is about 35% of the original length, but it could be summarised further.

■   **(d) Summarise the summary in no more than 20 words.**

5 Practice C

■ Summarise the following text in about 50 words.

THE LAST WORD IN LAVATORIES?

Toto is a leading Japanese manufacturer of bathroom ceramic ware, with annual worldwide sales of around $5 bn. One of its best-selling ranges is the Washlet lavatory, priced at up to $5,000 and used in most Japanese homes. This has features such as a heated seat, and can play a range of sounds. This type of toilet is successful in its home market since many flats are small and crowded, and bathrooms provide valued privacy. Now Toto hopes to increase its sales in Europe and America, where it faces a variety of difficulties. European countries tend to have their own rules about lavatory design, so that different models have to be made for each market. Although Toto claims that its Washlet design uses less water than the average model, one factor which may restrict its penetration into Europe is its need for an electrical socket for installation, as these are prohibited in bathrooms by most European building regulations.

---

6 Paraphrasing

Paraphrasing and summarising are normally used together in essay writing, but while summarising aims to **reduce** information to a suitable length, paraphrasing attempts to **restate** the relevant information. For example, the following sentence:

> *There has been much debate about the reasons for the Industrial Revolution happening in eighteenth-century Britain, rather than in France or Germany.*

could be paraphrased:

> *Why the Industrial Revolution occurred in the UK in the eighteenth century, instead of on the continent, has been the subject of considerable discussion.*

Note that an effective paraphrase usually:

* has a different structure to the original
* has mainly different vocabulary
* retains the same meaning
* keeps some phrases from the original that are in common use (e.g. 'Industrial Revolution' or 'eighteenth century').

7 Practice D

■ Read the text below and then evaluate the three paraphrases (1 = best), giving reasons.

THE CAUSES OF THE INDUSTRIAL REVOLUTION

Allen (2009) argues that the best explanation for the British location of the industrial revolution is found by studying demand factors. By the early eighteenth century high wages and cheap energy were both features of the British economy. Consequently, the mechanisation of industry through such inventions as the steam engine and mechanical spinning was profitable because employers were able to economise on labour by spending on coal. At that time, no other country had this particular combination of expensive labour and abundant fuel.

(a) A focus on demand may help to explain the UK origin of the Industrial Revolution. At that time, workers' pay was high, but energy from coal was inexpensive. This encouraged the development of mechanical inventions based on steam power, which enabled bosses to save money by mechanising production (Allen, 2009).

(b) The reason why Britain was the birthplace of the Industrial Revolution can be understood by analysing demand in the early 1700s, according to Allen (2009). He maintains that, uniquely, Britain had the critical combination of cheap energy from coal and high labour costs. This encouraged the adoption of steam power to mechanise production, thus saving on wages and increasing profitability.

(c) Allen (2009) claims that the clearest explanation for the UK location of the Industrial Revolution is seen by examining demand factors. By the eighteenth century, cheap energy and high wages were both aspects of the British economy. As a result, the mechanisation of industry through inventions such as the steam engine and mechanical spinning was profitable because employers were able to save money on labour by spending on coal. At that time, Britain was the only country with significant deposits of coal.

(1) _____

_____

(2) _____

_____

(3) _____

_____

8 Techniques for paraphrasing

(a) Changing vocabulary by using synonyms:

argues > claims/eighteenth century > 1700s/wages > labour costs/economise > saving

(b) Changing word class:

explanation (n.) > explain (v.)/mechanical (adj.) > mechanise (v.)/profitable (adj.) > profitability (n.)

(c) Changing word order:

. . . the best explanation for the British location of the industrial revolution is found by studying demand factors.

> A focus on demand may help explain the UK origin of the industrial revolution.

Note that in practice, all these three techniques are used at the same time. Do not attempt to paraphrase every word, since some have no true synonym (e.g. demand, economy).

▶ **See Units 3.3 Academic Vocabulary: Nouns and Adjectives, 3.4 Academic Vocabulary: Verbs and Adverbs and 3.9 Synonyms**

9 Practice E

■ Read the following text.

GREEN DREAMS?

It is often argued that governments can create employment and reduce carbon emissions by investing in renewable energy projects. These so-called 'green jobs' have the appeal of also helping to combat global warming while reducing a country's dependence on imported fuels. An American think-tank has calculated that the spending of $100 billion by the US government would result in the creation of two million jobs. A number of countries such as Germany, Spain and Indonesia have spent heavily on subsidising low-carbon technology.

However, critics of these schemes claim that the results are not as beneficial as they seem. Firstly, if the money was spent on other projects such as road building, jobs would also be created. Secondly, higher government borrowing to pay for the investment has to be financed by the taxpayer, and it may eventually affect the cost of borrowing for all businesses. In addition, subsidising relatively inefficient energy sources such as solar and wind power will raise the price of electricity for consumers.

A study in Spain looked at the cost of subsidising renewable energy over 25 years. The estimated expenditure of €29 billion will provide 50,000 jobs, but they will have cost €570,000 each to create. If, however, the government had allowed private industry to spend the same amount, it would have created 113,000 posts; more than twice as many. So it can be argued that the Spanish scheme will have actually destroyed over 50,000 jobs. Although these figures ignore both the environmental benefits and advantages for Spain of reducing demand for imported fossil fuels, it is clear that such green schemes do not automatically bring benefits to all.

■ **(a) Find synonyms for the words underlined. Rewrite the sentences using these.**

It is <u>often argued</u> that governments can create <u>employment</u> and <u>reduce</u> carbon emissions by investing in renewable energy <u>projects</u>. These so-called 'green jobs' have the <u>appeal</u> of also helping to <u>combat</u> global warming while <u>reducing</u> a <u>country's</u> dependence on imported fuels.

■ **(b) Change the word class of the underlined words. Rewrite the sentences using the changes.**

However, critics of these schemes <u>claim</u> that the results are not as <u>beneficial</u> as they seem. Firstly, if the money was <u>spent</u> on other projects such as road building, jobs would also be <u>created</u>.

■ **(c) Change the word order of these sentences, rewriting the paragraph so the meaning stays the same.**

Secondly, higher government borrowing to pay for the investment has to be financed by the taxpayer, and it may eventually affect the cost of borrowing for all businesses. In addition, subsidising relatively inefficient energy sources such as solar and wind power will raise the price of electricity for consumers.

■ **(d) Combine all three techniques to paraphrase the next paragraph.**

A study in Spain looked at the cost of subsidising renewable energy over 25 years. The estimated expenditure of €29 billion will provide 50,000 jobs, but they will have cost €570,000 each to create. If, however, the government had allowed private industry to spend the same amount, it would have created 113,000 posts; more than twice as many. So it can be argued that the Spanish scheme will have actually destroyed over 50,000 jobs.

10 Vocabulary revision

■   (a) The following verbs occurred in this unit. Find the corresponding noun.

transform	*transformation*
assess	
economise	
subsidise	
impede	
translate	

■   (b) The following nouns occurred in this unit. Find the corresponding verb.

innovation	
correlation	
replacement	
installation	
mechanisation	
dependence	

References and Quotations

Academic work involves using the research and ideas of others, so it is vital to show which sources you have used in your work, in an acceptable manner. This unit explains:

- the format of in-text citations
- the use of quotations
- the layout of lists of references.

1 Why use references?

There are three principal reasons for providing references:

(a) To show that you have read some of the authorities on the subject, which will give added weight to your writing.

(b) To allow the reader to find the source, if he/she wishes to examine the topic in more detail.

(c) To avoid plagiarism.

▶ **See Unit 1.3 Avoiding Plagiarism**

■ Decide if you need to give a reference in the following cases.

Academic situation	Yes/No
(a) Data you found from your own primary research	
(b) A graph from an internet article	
(c) A quotation from a book	
(d) An item of common knowledge	
(e) A theory from a journal article	
(f) An idea of your own based on reading several sources	

2 Citations and references

It is important to refer correctly to the work of other writers that you have used. You may present these sources as either a summary/paraphrase, as a quotation, or use both. In each case, a citation is included to provide a link to the list of references at the end of your paper.

■   **Underline the citations in the following examples. Which is a summary and which a quotation? What are the advantages of each?**

(a)   Friedman (1974) pointed out that inflation was effectively a kind of taxation.

(b)   As Friedman stated: 'Inflation is the one form of taxation that can be imposed without legislation' (1974: 93).

3 Reference verbs and systems

Summaries and quotations are usually introduced by a reference verb:

> *Friedman (1974)* **pointed out** *that* . . .

These verbs can be either in the present or the past tense. Normally, the use of the present tense suggests that the source is recent and still valid, while the past indicates that the source is older and may be out of date, but there are no hard-and-fast distinctions; Friedman's statement still has validity today.

There are several systems of referencing in use in the academic world, but most business schools use the Harvard system, which is explained here. You should ask your teachers if you are not sure which to use. With any system, the most important point is to be consistent (e.g. to use the same font size, punctuation, etc. throughout.

▶   **See Unit 3.4 Academic Vocabulary: Verbs and Adverbs (2 Using verbs of reference)**

4 Using quotations

Using a quotation means bringing the original words of a writer into your work. Quotations are effective in some situations, but must not be overused. They can be valuable:

- when the original words express an idea in a distinctive way
- when the original is more concise than your summary could be
- when the original version is well known (as in the quote from Friedman in section 2).

All quotations should be introduced by a phrase that shows the source, and also explains how this quotation fits into your argument:

Introductory phrase	Author	Reference verb	Quotation	Citation
This view is widely shared;	as Friedman	stated:	'Inflation is the one form of taxation that can be imposed without legislation'	(1974: 93).

(a) Short quotations (two to three lines) are shown by single quotation marks. Quotations inside quotations (nested quotations) use double quotation marks:

   As James remarked: 'Martin's concept of "internal space" requires close analysis.'

(b) Longer quotations are either indented (given a wider margin) and/or are printed in smaller type.

(c) Page numbers should be given after the date.

(d) Care must be taken to ensure that quotations are the exact words of the original. If it is necessary to delete some words that are irrelevant, use points (. . .) to show where the missing section was:

   'Few inventions . . . have been as significant as the mobile phone.'

(e) It may be necessary to insert a word or phrase into the quotation to clarify a point. This can be done by using square brackets ([ ]):

   '[this second category of] products is distinguished by its high brand recognition and resistance to switching strategies . . .'

5 Practice

■ Study the following paragraph from an article called 'The mobile revolution' in the journal *Development Quarterly* (Issue 34, pages 85–97, 2009) by K. Hoffman. Then compare the summary and quotation.

According to recent estimates there are at least 4 billion mobile phones in the world, and the majority of these are owned by people in the developing world. Ownership in the developed world reached saturation level by 2007, so countries such as China, India and Brazil now account for most of the growth. In the poorest countries, with weak transport networks and unreliable postal services, access to telecommunications is a vital tool for starting or developing a business, since it provides access to wider markets. Studies have shown that when household incomes rise, more money is spent on mobile phones than any other item.

(a) *Summary*
Hoffman (2009) stresses the critical importance in the developing world of mobile phones in the growth of small businesses.

(b) *Quotation*
According to Hoffman, mobile phone ownership compensates for the weaknesses of infrastructure in the developing world: 'In the poorest countries, with weak transport networks and unreliable postal services, access to telecommunications is a vital tool for starting or developing a business, since it provides access to wider markets' (2009: 87).

(c) *Summary and quotation*
Hoffman points out that most of the growth in mobile phone ownership now takes place in the developing world, where it has become crucial for establishing a business: '. . . access to telecommunications is a vital tool for starting or developing a business, since it provides access to wider markets' (2009: 87).

■ **Read the next paragraph of the same article.**

In such countries the effect of phone ownership on GDP growth is much stronger than in the developed world, because the ability to make calls is being offered for the first time, rather than as an alternative to existing landlines. As a result, mobile phone operators have emerged in Africa, India and other parts of Asia that are larger and more flexible than Western companies, and which have grown by catering for poorer customers, being therefore well-placed to expand downmarket. In addition Chinese phone makers have successfully challenged the established Western companies in terms of quality as well as innovation. A further trend is the provision of services via the mobile network which offer access to information about healthcare or agricultural advice.

■   (a) Write a summary of the main point, including a citation.

■   (b) Introduce a quotation to show the key point, referring to the source.

■   (c) Combine (a) and (b), again acknowledging the source.

6 Abbreviations in citations

In-text citations use the following abbreviations, derived from Latin and printed in italics:

*   *et al.*: Used when three or more authors are given. The full list of names is given in the reference list
*   ibid.: Taken from the same source (i.e. the same page) as the previous citation.
*   *op. cit.*: Taken from the same source as previously, but a different page.

Note that journal articles increasingly tend to use full citations, but students should still use the above in their work.

▶   **See 3.2 Abbreviations**

7 Secondary references

It is quite common to find a reference to an original source in the text you are reading.

For instance, if you are reading a text by McArthur, you may find:

> *Chan (2012) argues that there was a significant change in management style between 1985 and the end of the century.*

You may wish to use this information from the original (i.e. Chan) in your writing, even if you have not read the whole work. This is known as a secondary reference. If it is not possible to locate the original, you can refer to it thus:

> *Chan (2012), cited in McArthur (2014: 241), maintained that there was an important change . . .*

You must include the work you have read (i.e. McArthur) in the list of references.

8 Organising the list of references

> There are many software systems available (e.g. RefWorks or Endnote) that automate the making of a list of references. Using one of them not only saves time, but may also help to produce a more accurate result. Some are free and others require payment, but if you search your library website you may find one that you can access without charge.

At the end of an essay or report, there must be a list of all the sources cited in the writing. Note that the list is organised alphabetically by the family name of the author. You should be clear about the difference between first names and family names. On title pages, the normal format of first name then family name is used:

Sheila Burford, Juan Gonzalez

But in citations, only the family name is usually used:

Burford (2001), Gonzalez (1997)

In reference lists, use the family name and the first initial:

Burford, S., Gonzalez, J.

If you are not sure which name is the family name, ask a classmate from that cultural background.

■ **Study the reference list below and answer the following questions.**

REFERENCES

Brander, J. and Spencer, B. (1985) 'Export subsidies and international market share rivalry'. *Journal of International Economics* 18, 83–100.

Cable, V. (1983) *Protectionism and Industrial Decline.* London: Hodder & Stoughton.

Conrad, K. (1989) 'Productivity and cost gaps in manufacturing industries in US, Japan and Germany'. *European Economic Review* 33, 1135–1159.

Gribben, R. (2009) 'Ministers accelerate support for car industry'. *The Daily Telegraph* online. Downloaded from: www.telegraph.co.uk/finance/newsbysector/transport/4975676/Ministers-accelerate-support-for-car-industry.html [12 March 2009].

Intriligator, M. (2005) 'Globalisation of the world economy: potential benefits and costs and a net assessment' in Gangopadhyay, R. and Chatterji, M. (eds) *Economics of Globalisation*. Aldershot: Ashgate, 67–76.

OECD (1998) *Open Markets Matter: The benefits of trade and investment liberalisation*. Paris: OECD.

Runciman, K. and Jenner, F. (2013) *New Markets for Old: The Inside Story of Globalisation*. New York: Curtis & Bloomberg.

The Economist (2009) 'Underpowered'. 16 April. Downloaded from: www.economist.com/world/britain/displaystory.cfm?story_id=13497452 [29 April 2009].

(a) Find an example of:

    (i)   a book by one author

    (ii) a journal article

    (iii) a chapter in an edited book

    (iv) an article from a newspaper website

    (v)   an anonymous magazine article (electronic)

    (vi) an official report

(b) What are the main differences in the way these sources are referenced?

    (i)   _____

    (ii) _____

    (iii) _____

    (iv) _____

    (v)   _____

    (vi) _____

(c) When are italics used?

(d) How are capital letters used in titles?

(e) How is a source with no given author listed?

(f)   Write citations for summaries from each of the sources.

(i)   _____

(ii)   _____

(iii)   _____

(iv)   _____

(v)   _____

(vi)   _____

(vii)   _____

(viii)   _____

▶   For a full guide to the use of the Harvard system see:
    http://home.ched.coventry.ac.uk/caw/harvard/

Combining Sources

For most assignments, students are expected to read a range of sources, often reflecting conflicting views on a topic. In some cases, the contrast between the various views may be the focus of the task. This unit explains how a writer can present and organise a range of contrasting sources.

1 Mentioning sources

In the early stages of an essay, it is common to discuss the contribution of other writers to the subject.

■ Read the following example, from a comparison of 'technology readiness' in Chinese and American consumers, and answer the questions opposite.

The extent to which consumers desire to use new technology is commonly influenced by factors such as consumer attitudes toward specific technologies (Bobbit and Dabholkar, 2001; Curran *et al.*, 2003), the level of technology anxiety exhibited by consumers (Meuter, Ostrom, Bitner and Roundtree, 2003), and consumer capacity and willingness (Walker, Lees, Hecker and Francis, 2002). Mick and Fournier (1998) argue that consumers can simultaneously exhibit positive feelings (such as intelligence and efficacy) and negative feelings (such as ignorance and ineptitude) towards new technology. Venkatesh (2000) found that 'computer playfulness' and 'computer anxiety' serve as anchors that users employ in forming perceptions of ease of use about new technology.

(a) How many sources are mentioned here?

(b) What was the subject of Meuter, Ostrom, Bitner and Roundtree's research?

(c) Which source contrasted fear of computers with playing with computers?

(d) Which source examined the paradox of positive and negative attitudes to computers?

(e) How many sources are cited that studied attitudes to particular technologies?

▶ **See Unit 4.3 Literature Reviews**

2 Taking a critical approach

It is important to compare a range of views to show that you are familiar with different and conflicting views on a topic. This is because most topics worth studying are the subject of debate. The two texts below reflect different approaches to the topic of globalisation.

■ **Read them both and then study the extract from an introduction to an essay that mentions the two sources. Answer the questions that follow.**

GLOBALISATION

1

It has been claimed that globalisation is not a new phenomenon, but has its roots in the age of colonial development in the seventeenth and eighteenth centuries. However, its modern use can be dated to 1983, when Levitt's article 'The Globalisation of Markets' was published. Among the many definitions of the process that have been suggested, perhaps the simplest is that globalisation is the relatively free movement of services, goods, people and ideas world-wide. An indication of the positive effect of the process is that cross-border world trade, as a percentage of global GDP, was 15% in 1990 but is expected to reach 30% by 2015. Among the forces driving globalisation in the last two decades have been market liberalisation, cheap communication via the internet and telephony, and the growth of the BRIC (Brazil, Russia, India and China) economies.

(Costa, L., 2008)

GLOBALISATION

2

Considerable hostility to the forces of globalisation has been demonstrated in both the developed and developing worlds. In the former, there is anxiety about the outsourcing of manufacturing and service jobs to countries which offer cheaper labour, while developing countries claim that only a minority have benefited from the increase in world trade. They point out that per-capita income in the 20 poorest countries has hardly changed in the past 40 years, while in the richest 20 it has tripled. The markets of Western nations are still closed to agricultural products from developing countries, and while there is free movement of goods and capital, migration from poor countries to rich ones is tightly controlled.

(Lin, Y., 2006)

ESSAY EXTRACT

Costa (2008) argues that globalisation, although not a modern phenomenon, has recently accelerated, encouraged by forces such as the liberalisation of markets and cheap communication. In particular, it has had a powerful effect in increasing world trade, especially benefiting the BRIC economies such as Brazil and China. However, Lin (2006) emphasises the negative reactions that have been produced by the process. She highlights the fears of unemployment in richer nations created by outsourcing work, matched by the concerns of poorer states that they are not sharing in the economic growth due to barriers to their trade and labour.

■ (a) The extract summarises ideas from both Costa and Lin. Find an example of a summary in the extract and match it with the original text in 1 or 2.

Summary	Original

■ (b) Which verbs are used to introduce the summaries?

■ (c) Which word marks the point where the writer switches from considering Costa to dealing with Lin?

■ (d) What other words or phrases could be used at this point?

3 Practice

■ Read the third text on globalisation below, and then complete the paragraph from an essay titled: 'Globalisation mainly benefits multinational companies rather than ordinary people – discuss', using all three sources.

Multi-national companies have undoubtedly benefited from the relaxation of the import tariff regimes which previously protected local firms, allowing them to operate more freely in markets such as India which have recently liberalised. These corporations have evolved two distinct approaches to the challenge of globalisation. Some, e.g. Gillette, have continued to produce their products in a few large plants with strict control to ensure uniform quality, while others, for instance Coca-Cola, vary the product to suit local tastes and tend to manufacture their goods on the spot. They claim that an understanding of regional differences is essential for competing with national rivals.

(Brokaw, P., 2002)

Lin (2006) demonstrates that globalisation has benefited the multinationals that have transferred production from . . .

4 Vocabulary revision

■   Match the words and phrases found in this unit (on the left) with their meanings on the right.

Simultaneously	Locally
Ineptitude	Certainly improved
Cross-border world trade	Tax on goods entering countries
Outsourcing	Poor ability
Undoubtedly benefited	Variation between areas
Import tariff regimes	Strictly regulated
Uniform quality	At the same time
On the spot	Buying and selling between countries
Regional differences	Moving production or services abroad
Tightly controlled	Regular standard

Organising Paragraphs

Paragraphs are the basic building blocks of academic writing. Well structured paragraphs help the reader to understand the topic more easily by dividing up the argument into convenient sections. This unit looks at:

- the components of paragraphs
- the way the components are linked together
- the linkage between paragraphs in the overall text.

1 Paragraph structure

■ Discuss the following questions with a partner.

- What is a paragraph?
- What is the normal length of a paragraph?
- Is there a standard structure for paragraphs?
- How is a paragraph linked together?

2 Example paragraph

■ Study the paragraph below. It is from the introduction to an essay titled 'Should home ownership be encouraged?'.

> The rate of home ownership varies widely across the developed world. Germany, for instance, has one of the lowest rates, at 42%, while in Spain it is twice as high, 85%. Both the USA and Britain have similar rates of about 69%. The reasons for this variation appear to be more cultural and historic than economic, since high rates are found in both rich and poorer countries. There appears to be no conclusive link between national prosperity and the number of home owners.

The paragraph can be analysed:

1 Topic sentence	The rate of home ownership varies widely across the developed world.
2 Example 1	Germany, **for instance**, has one of the lowest rates, at 42%, **while** in Spain it is twice as high, 85%.
3 Example 2	Both the USA and Britain have similar rates of about 69%.
4 Reason	**The reasons for** this variation appear to be more cultural and historic than economic, **since** high rates are found in both rich and poorer countries.
5 Summary	**There appears to be** no conclusive link between national prosperity and the number of home owners.

This example shows that:

(a) A paragraph is a group of sentences that deal with a single topic.

(b) The length of paragraphs varies significantly according to text type, but should generally be no less than four or five sentences.

(c) Normally (but not always), the first sentence introduces the topic. Other sentences may give definitions, examples, information, reasons, restatements and summaries.

(d) The parts of the paragraph are linked together by the phrases and conjunctions shown in bold in the table. They guide the reader through the argument presented.

▶ **See Unit 3.5 Conjunctions**

3 Practice A

■ Read the next paragraph from the same essay and answer the questions below.

> Despite this, many countries encourage the growth of home ownership. Ireland and Spain, for example, allow mortgage payers to offset payments against income tax. It is widely believed that owning your own home has social as well as economic benefits. Compared to renters, home owners are thought to be more stable members of the community who contribute more to local affairs. In addition, neighbourhoods of owner occupiers are considered to have less crime and better schools. But above all, ownership encourages saving and allows families to build wealth.

	Despite this, many countries encourage the growth of home ownership.
	Ireland and Spain, for example, allow mortgage payers to offset payments against income tax.
	It is widely believed that owning your own home has social as well as economic benefits.
Supporting point 1	Compared to renters, home owners are thought to be more stable members of the community who contribute more to local affairs.
	In addition, neighbourhoods of owner occupiers are considered to have less crime and better schools.
	But above all, ownership encourages saving and allows families to build wealth.

■ (a) Analyse the paragraph by completing the left-hand column in the table above with the following types of sentence: Supporting point 1, Supporting point 2, Supporting point 3, Example, Reason, Topic.

■ (b) Underline the words and phrases used to link the sentences together.

■ (c) Which phrase is used to link this paragraph to the one before?

4 Development of ideas

■ (a) The sentences below form the third paragraph of the same essay, but they have been mixed up. Use the table below to put them in the correct order.

(i)   When this burst, millions of people lost their homes, which for many had contained their savings.

(ii)   These had been developed to allow higher-risk poorer families to buy their own homes, but contributed to a property price bubble.

(iii) Many economists now argue that there is a maximum level of home ownership which should not be exceeded.

(iv)   All these claims were challenged by the economic crash of 2008, which was in large part caused by defaults on American sub-prime mortgages.

(v)   Even households which had positive equity still felt poorer and reduced their spending.

(vi)   Others were trapped in their houses by negative equity, in other words their houses were worth less than they had paid for them.

Topic sentence	
Definition	
Result 1	
Result 2	
Result 3	
Conclusion	

■ (b) Underline the phrase used to link the paragraph to the previous one.

■ (c) Underline the words and phrases used to link the paragraph together.

5 Introducing paragraphs and linking them together

In order to begin a new topic you may use phrases such as:

Turning to the issue of . . .

Inflation must also be examined . . .

. . . is another area for consideration

Paragraphs can also be introduced with adverbs:

Traditionally, few examples were . . .

Finally, the performance of . . .

Currently, there is little evidence of . . .

In the essay on home ownership above, each new paragraph begins with a phrase that links it to the previous paragraph, in order to maintain continuity of argument:

Despite this (i.e. the lack of a conclusive link)

All these claims (i.e. arguments in favour of home ownership)

6 Practice B

■ Use the notes below to write an introductory paragraph of an essay titled: 'High rates of home ownership are bad for the economy – discuss'.

• It is claimed that increases in rate of home ownership lead to unemployment

• Home ownership appears to make people more reluctant to move to find work

• e.g. Spain (high ownership + high unemployment) vs. Switzerland (low ownership + low unemployment)

• Theory still controversial – other factors have been proposed

• e.g. liquidity of housing markets (how easy to sell houses)

1	*It has been argued that a rise in the rate of home ownership can increase the rate of unemployment.*
2	
3	
4	
5	

7 Practice C

■ Use the information below to write a paragraph about Bill Gates.

1955   Bill Gates was born, the second child in a middle-class Seattle family

1968   At age 13, he became interested in writing computer programmes

1975   Gates and his school friend Allen started a programming business called Microsoft

1980   IBM asked Microsoft to write operating system (called MS-DOS) for its new PC

1985   Microsoft launched Windows operating system

1995   Gates became the richest man in world

2006   He stepped down from working at Microsoft to focus on his charitable foundation

8 Vocabulary revision

■ (a) Decide if the following are nouns or adjectives, and then complete the table with the missing words.

- liquidity
- reluctant
- stable
- prosperity
- controversial
- conclusive

Nouns	Adjectives
liquidity	*liquid*

■ **(b) Explain the meaning of the following terms to a partner.**

- default
- sub-prime mortgage
- housing bubble
- income tax
- negative equity

Introductions and Conclusions

An effective introduction explains the purpose and scope of the paper to the reader. The conclusion should provide a clear answer to any question asked in the title, as well as summarising the main points. In coursework, both introductions and conclusions are normally written after the main body.

1 Introduction contents

Introductions are usually no more than about 10% of the total length of the assignment. Therefore, in a 2,000-word essay, the introduction would be about 200 words.

■ (a) What is normally found in an essay introduction? Choose from the list below.

Components	Yes/No
(i) A definition of any unfamiliar terms in the title	
(ii) The conclusions you reached on the topic	
(iii) Mention of some sources you have read on the topic	
(iv) A provocative idea or question to interest the reader	
(v) Your aim or purpose in writing	
(vi) The method you adopt to answer the question (or an outline)	
(vii) Some background to the topic	
(viii) Any limitations you set yourself	

■ **(b) Read the extracts below from introductions to articles and decide which of the components listed opposite they illustrate.**

(i) The goal of the present study is to complement the existing body of knowledge on HR practices with a large scale empirical study, and at the same time contribute to the discussion on why some firms are more innovative than others.

(ii) We consider three dimensions of customer satisfaction: service, quality and price. We argue that employees most directly influence customer satisfaction with service. We test this proposition empirically, and then examine the links between customer satisfaction and sales.

(iii) Corporate governance is a set of mechanisms, both institutional and market-based, designed to mitigate agency problems that arise from the separation of ownership and control in a company, protect the interests of all stakeholders, improve from performance and ensure that investors get an adequate return on their investment.

(iv) This study will focus on mergers in the media business between 1990 and 2009, since with more recent examples an accurate assessment of the consequences cannot yet be made.

(v) The rest of the paper is organised as follows. The second section explains why corporate governance is important for economic prosperity. The third section presents the model specification and describes the data and variables used in our empirical analysis. The fourth section reports and discusses the empirical results. The fifth section concludes.

(vi) The use of incentive compensation, such as bonus and stock options, is an important means of motivating and compensating executives of private companies, especially executives of technology-orientated companies.

(vii) There is no clear empirical evidence sustaining a 'managerial myopia' argument. Pugh *et al.* (1992) find evidence that supports such theory, but Meulbrook *et al.* (1990), Mahoney *et al.* (1997), Garvey and Hanka (1999) and a study by the Office of the Chief Economist of the Securities and Exchange Commission (1985) find no evidence.

2 Introduction structure

Not every introduction will include all the elements listed above.

■ **Decide which are essential and which are optional.**

There is no standard pattern for an introduction, since much depends on the type of research you are conducting and the length of your work, but a common framework is:

(a)	Definition of key terms, if needed
(b)	Relevant background information
(c)	Review of work by other writers on the topic
(d)	Purpose or aim of the paper
(e)	Your methods
(f)	Any limitations you imposed
(g)	The organisation of your work

(a) Certain words or phrases in the title may need clarifying because they are not widely understood.

   For the purpose of this paper, I define serendipity as search leading to unintended discovery.

► **See Unit 2.6 Definitions**

(b) It is useful to remind the reader of the wider context of your work. This may also show the importance and value of the study you have carried out.

   A major strength of this study is the theoretically informed context-embedded selection of HR practices in explaining why some firms are more innovative than others.

(c) While a longer article may have a separate literature review, in a shorter essay it is still important to show familiarity with researchers who have studied this topic previously.

   The last few years have, indeed, witnessed many notable interventions and seminal articulations of the pros and cons of globalisation for perceived disadvantaged groups, including workers (Haq, 2003; Horgan, 2001; Klein, 2000; Rai, 2001).

(d) The aim of your research must be clearly stated so the reader is clear what you are trying to do.

   The key question addressed in this study is a simple one: Is innovativeness a link between pay and performance in the technology sector?

(e) The method demonstrates the process that you undertook to achieve the aim given previously.

   Using a sample of 988 Dutch firms, the relationship between a set of six HR practices and the fraction of radically and incrementally changed products in a firm's total sales is explored.

(f)   Clearly, you cannot deal with every aspect of the topic in an essay, so you must make clear the boundaries of your study.

The focus will be on corporate governance in South Asian companies.

(g)   Understanding the structure of your work will help the reader to follow your argument.

The paper deals with these points as follows. The first section describes the concept of serendipity and offers a framework that integrates serendipity within the entrepreneurship literature. The following section discusses . . .

3 Opening sentences

It can be difficult to start writing an essay, but especially in exams, hesitation will waste valuable time. The first few sentences should be general but not vague, to help the reader focus on the topic. They often have the following pattern:

Time phrase	Topic	Development
Currently,	marketing theory	is being reassessed.
Since 2008,	electric vehicles	have become a serious commercial proposition.

It is important to avoid opening sentences that are overly general. Compare:

Nowadays, there is a lot of competition among different providers of news.	✗
Newspapers are currently facing strong competition from rival news providers such as the internet and television.	✓

■   **Write introductory sentences for three of the following titles.**

(a)   How important is it for companies to have women as senior managers?

(b)   What are the 'pull' factors in international tourism?

(c)   What is the relationship between inflation and unemployment?

(d)   'Monopolies are inefficient in using resources' – discuss.

▶   **See Unit 2.8 Generalisations**

4 Practice A

You have to write an essay titled 'State control of industry: does it have any benefits?'.

■ Using the notes below and your own ideas, write a short introduction for the essay (it is not necessary to refer to sources in this exercise).

<u>Definition</u> – state control = public ownership, especially of 'natural monopoly' industries (e.g. electricity, water supply)

<u>Background</u> – worldwide trend to privatise industries but subject to controversy (e.g. postal service, railways)

<u>Aim</u> – to establish what advantages may come from public ownership of these industries

<u>Method</u> – compare advantages (security of supply, benefits of large-scale operation) and disadvantages (lack of competition, corruption, political control) in UK and France, in two industries: railways and electricity

<u>Limitation</u> – 1995–2010

5 Conclusions

Conclusions tend to be shorter and more varied in format than introductions. Some articles may have a 'summary' or 'concluding remarks'. But student papers should generally have a final section that summarises the arguments and makes it clear to the reader that the original question has been answered.

■ Which of the following are generally acceptable in conclusions?

(a) A statement showing how your aim has been achieved.

(b) A discussion of the implications of your research.

(c) Some new information on the topic not mentioned before.

(d) A short review of the main points of your study.

(e) Some suggestions for further research.

(f) Mention of the limitations of your study.

(g) Comparison with the results of similar studies.

(h) A quotation that appears to sum up your work.

■ Match the extracts from conclusions below with the acceptable components opposite (example: a = vi).

(i)   As always, this investigation has a number of limitations to be considered in evaluating its findings.

(ii) Obviously, business expatriates could benefit from being informed that problem-focused coping strategies are more effective than symptom-focused ones.

(iii) Another line of research worth pursuing further is to study the importance of language for expatriate assignments.

(iv) Our review of 13 studies of strikes in public transport demonstrates that the effect of a strike on public transport ridership varies and may either be temporary or permanent.

(v)   These results of the Colombia study reported here are consistent with other similar studies conducted in other countries (Baron and Norman, 1992).

(vi) This study has clearly illustrated the drawbacks to family ownership of retail businesses.

6 Practice B

■ Look at Unit 1.9 Organising Paragraphs, sections 2, 3 and 4. Study the first three paragraphs of the essay (Should home ownership be encouraged?), then write a concluding paragraph of about 100 words that summarises the main points and answers the question in the title.

Rewriting and Proofreading

In exams, you have no time for rewriting, but for coursework it is important to take time to revise your work to improve its clarity and logical development. In both situations, proofreading is essential to avoid the small errors that may make your work inaccurate or even difficult to understand.

1 Rewriting

Although it is tempting to think that the first draft of an essay is adequate, it is almost certain that it can be improved. After completing your first draft, you should leave it for a day and then reread it, asking yourself the following questions:

(a) Does this fully answer the question(s) in the title?
(b) Do the different sections of the paper have the right weight (i.e. is it well balanced)?
(c) Does the argument or discussion develop clearly and logically?
(d) Have I forgotten any important points that would support the development?

2 Practice A

You have written the first draft of a 2,000-word essay titled: 'Assess the relevance of motivation theories for today's managers in assisting them to increase employee performance, using the case of a Japanese car producer operating in the UK.'

■ Study the introduction to this essay opposite and decide how it could be improved, listing your suggestions in the table.

In the modern commercial society of today, the success of companies does not just rely on the external business environment, but more importantly depends on the internal management of human resources, due to the inseparable relationship between employee performance and the achievement of companies. Thus, the employees play a significant role in the development of companies, and their performance is determined by ability, work environment and motivation. Nowadays, organisations pay increasing attention to the importance of motivating employees. This essay will present a clear theoretical framework of work motivation, and then concentrate on evaluating the empirical relevance of those theories.

	Suggestions for improvement
(a)	*Rather short (100 words) for introduction to a 2,000-word essay*
(b)	
(c)	
(d)	
(e)	

With these points in mind, the introduction could be rewritten as follows:

In the current commercial environment, the success of companies does not just rely on the external business climate, but more importantly depends on the internal management of human resources, due to the inseparable relationship between employee performance and the achievement of companies (Agarwala, 2003). Clearly, the employees play a significant role in the development and achievements of companies, and their performance is determined by ability, work environment and motivation (Griffin, 1990).

Consequently, employee motivation is an increasingly important concern for companies. This essay will first present a clear theoretical framework of work motivation, focusing first on Maslow's hierarchy of needs theory and Herzberg's two-factor theory. The second section will concentrate on evaluating the empirical relevance of those theories to the modern workplace, by analysing the measures taken by the Japanese car producer Toyota to motivate its British employees. This study is confined to the period from 1998 to 2012, as these are the latest years for which accurate data can be obtained.

3 Practice B

■   **Read the draft conclusion to the same essay and decide how it could be improved. Rewrite the conclusion.**

To conclude, it has been shown that the hierarchy of needs theory of Maslow, Herzberg's two-factor theory and the achievement theory of McClelland have some relevance to the motivation of British employees. The application of these theories has sometimes resulted in increased employee performance. Some limitations to the application of these theories have been demonstrated. Cross-cultural problems have arisen. Knowledge workers need different motivation methods. The older theories of motivation are not always relevant to today's workplace. This kind of organisational experience needs a more up-to-date theoretical basis.

4 Proofreading

(a) Proofreading means checking your work for small errors that may make it more difficult for the reader to understand exactly what you want to say. If a sentence has only one error:

She has no enough interpersonal skills to handle different relationships.

it is not difficult to understand, but if there are multiple errors, even though they are all quite minor, the effect is very confusing:

As keynes, the Bitish economic, siad, 'In the long run . . .. we are all ded'.

Clearly, you should aim to make your meaning as clear as possible. Note that computer spellchecks do not always help you, since they may ignore a word that is spelt correctly but is not the word you meant to use:

Tow factors need to be considered . . .

■   (b) Examples of the most common types of error in student writing are shown below. In each case, underline the error and correct it.

(i)   Factual: *Corruption is a problem in many countries such as Africa.*

(ii)   Word ending: *She was young and innocence . . .*

(iii) Punctuation: *What is the optimum size for a family business*

(iv)   Tense: *Until the early 1980s, there were about 15 assemblers that produce vehicles . . .*

(v)   Vocabulary: *. . . vital to the successfulness of a company operating in China*

(vi)   Spelling: *Pervious experience can sometimes give researchers . . .*

(vii) Singular/plural: *One of the largest company in Asia.*

(viii) Style: *. . . finally, the essay will conclude with a conclusion.*

(ix)   Missing word: *An idea established by David Ricardo in nineteenth century.*

(x)   Word order: *A rule of marketing which states that consumers when go out shopping . . .*

■   (c) The following extracts each contain one type of error. Match each to one of the examples (i–x) above, and correct the error.

(i)   Products like Tiger biscuits are well-known to kids . . .

(ii)   Both companies focus on mass marketing to promote its line of products.

(iii) Failure to find the right product may lead to torment for consumers.

(iv)   . . . different researchers have differently effects on the research.

(v)   After the single European market was established in 1873 . . .

(vi)   . . . experienced researchers can most likely come over these problems.

(vii) Firstly because, it provides them with an opportunity for borrowing capital . . .

(viii) The company selected Budapest in Hungry for setting up its development centre.

(ix)   These cases demonstrate why companies from the rest of world are eager to . . .

(x)   Since 2009, few companies entered the French market . . .

5 Practice C

■ Underline the errors in the paragraph below and correct them.

Bicycle is one of most efficient machine ever designed. Cyclists can travel for times faster than walkers; when using less enorgy to do so. There were several early versions of the bicycle, but the first modle with pedals which was successful mass-produced was make by a frenchman, Ernest Michaux, on 1861. Later aditions included pneumatic tyres and gears. Today hundreds of million of bicycles are in use all over world.

Working in Groups

Many courses in business schools expect students to complete written tasks as part of a group of four to eight students. This unit explains the reasons for this, and suggests the best way to approach group work in order to achieve the maximum benefit from the process.

1 Group work

■ Read the text and complete the following exercise.

THE IMPORTANCE OF GROUP WORK IN THE BUSINESS SCHOOL

Some students in business schools, especially those from other academic cultures, may be surprised to find they are expected to work in groups to complete some academic assignments. For those who have always worked on their own this may cause a kind of culture shock, especially as all the students in the group will normally be given the same mark for the group's work. In addition, students are normally told who they will work with, although with some kinds of project the group may be able to choose its own topic. However, there are important reasons for this emphasis on group work in many English-speaking institutions.

First of all, employers are generally looking for people who can work in a team. Most managers are not looking for brilliant individuals, instead they want employees who are comfortable working with a mixed group with different skills and backgrounds. So familiarity with teamwork has become an essential qualification for many jobs, and this task provides students with an opportunity to strengthen their experience of working in groups.

Furthermore, working in groups allows individuals to achieve more than they could by working on their own. A group can tackle much larger projects, and this applies to most research projects at university, as well as business development in companies. Therefore, by taking part in these activities students are able to provide evidence on their portfolio and CV that they have succeeded in this critical area.

Working in pairs, decide if the following statements are true or false.

(a) Most students react positively to the idea of group work.

(b) All the group members receive the same mark.

(c) Students in groups can normally choose who they work with.

(d) There are two main reasons for setting group work.

(e) Most employers look for successful team members.

(f) Group work in business school has no connection to team work in companies.

2 Making group work successful

■ Below is a list of suggestions for making your group work successful. The correct order (1–7) has been mixed up. Working with a partner, put them into the most logical sequence, using the table.

Analyse the task

Get everyone to discuss the assignment and agree on the best methods to complete it. At this stage, it is important to have complete agreement on the objectives.

Divide up the work fairly, according to the abilities of the members

Your group may include a computer expert or a design genius, so make sure that their talents are used appropriately. It is most important to make sure that everyone feels they have been given a fair share of the work.

Make everyone feel included

Nobody should feel an outsider, so make special efforts if there is only one male student, or one non-native speaker, for instance. Make a list of all members' phone numbers and email addresses and give everyone a copy.

Finish the assignment on time

This is the most important test of your group's performance. When you have finished and handed in your work, it may be helpful to have a final meeting to discuss what you have all learned from the task.

Get to know the other members

Normally you cannot choose who you work with, so it is crucial to introduce yourselves before starting work. Meet informally in a café or similar (but be careful not to choose a meeting place that may make some members uncomfortable, such as a bar).

Select a coordinator/editor

Someone needs to take notes about what was agreed at meetings and send these to all members as a reminder. The same person could also act as editor, to make sure that all the individual sections conform to the same layout and format. However, you should all be responsible for proofreading your own work.

Plan the job and the responsibilities

Break down the task week by week and allocate specific roles to each member. Agree on times for regular meetings – although you may be able to avoid some meetings by using group emails. You may want to book a suitable room, for example in the library, to hold your meetings.

	Schedule – successful group work
1	Get to know the other members
2	
3	
4	
5	
6	
7	

3 Dealing with problems

■   Working in groups of three, discuss the best response to the following situations. You may choose an alternative strategy to the ones provided.

(a)   In a group of six, you find that two students are not doing any work. Not only do they not come to meetings, but they have not done the tasks they were given at the beginning. Should you . . .

   (i)   decide that it's simplest to do the work of the missing students yourself?

   (ii)   find the students and explain that their behaviour is going to damage the chances of all six members?

   (iii)   tell your lecturer about the problem?

(b) You are the only non-native speaker in the group. Although you can understand normal speech, the other students speak so fast and idiomatically that you have difficulty taking part in the discussions. Should you . . .

   (i)   tell your lecturer about the problem?

   (ii)   keep quiet and ask another student in the group to explain decisions later?

   (iii)   explain your problem to the group and ask them to speak more slowly?

(c)   One member of the group is very dominant. He/she attempts to control the group and is intolerant of the opinions of others. Should you . . .

   (i)   explain to them, in a group meeting, that their behaviour is having a negative effect on the group's task?

   (ii)   tell your lecturer about the problem?

   (iii)   let them do all the work, because that's what they seem to want?

4 Points to remember

Finally, remember that:

*   Working in groups is an ideal opportunity to make new friends – make the most of it.
*   You may learn a lot by listening to other people's ideas.
*   Negotiation is important in a group – nobody is right all the time.
*   Respect the values and attitudes of others, especially people from different cultures – you may be surprised what you learn.

Revision Exercise
The Writing Process

___

■ Study the flowchart below, which explains the process of writing an essay. Then complete the description of the process by adding one suitable word to each gap in the text on p. 86.

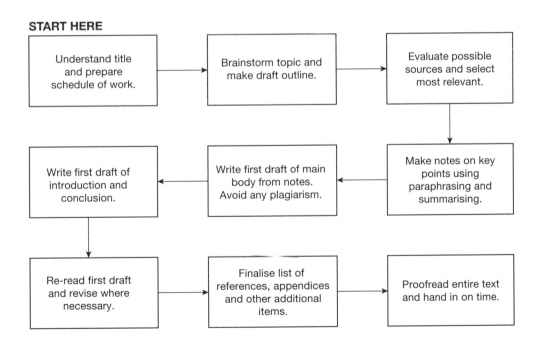

START HERE

Understand title and prepare schedule of work. → Brainstorm topic and make draft outline. → Evaluate possible sources and select most relevant.

Write first draft of introduction and conclusion. ← Write first draft of main body from notes. Avoid any plagiarism. ← Make notes on key points using paraphrasing and summarising.

Re-read first draft and revise where necessary. → Finalise list of references, appendices and other additional items. → Proofread entire text and hand in on time.

The first (a) _____ of essay writing is to read and understand

(b) _____ title, and then to prepare a schedule of work

(c) _____ the available time. Then the topic should be brainstormed

and a draft (d) _____ prepared. Next, possible (e) _____

have to be (f) _____ evaluated and the most relevant selected, after

(g) _____ you can start making notes, using paraphrasing and

(h) _____ techniques. When you have collected enough material to

(i) _____ the question, the first (j) _____ of the main body

can be written from the notes, taking care to (k) _____ any plagiarism.

Subsequently, you can write the first draft of the (l) _____ and

conclusion, making sure that a logical approach to the subject is developed.

(m) _____ this, the whole draft must be critically reread and

(n) _____ for clarity and relevance. The penultimate stage is

(o) _____ prepare a final (p) _____ of references and other

items such as tables and graphs. Finally, the whole text (q) _____ be

thoroughly (r) _____ before handing in the assignment on time.

Elements of Writing

UNIT
2.1
Argument and Discussion

On most courses, it is not enough to show that you are familiar with the leading authorities. Students are expected to study the conflicting views on any topic and engage with them, which means analysing and critiquing them if appropriate. This unit demonstrates ways of showing your familiarity with both sides of an argument and presenting your conclusions in a suitably academic manner.

1 Discussion vocabulary

Essay titles commonly ask students to 'discuss' a topic:

'Working from home can be positive for many companies and their employees – discuss.'

This requires an evaluation of both the benefits and disadvantages of the topic, with a section of the essay, sometimes headed 'Discussion', in which a summary of these is made. The following vocabulary can be used:

+	–
benefit	drawback
advantage	disadvantage
a positive aspect	a negative feature
pro (informal)	con (informal)
plus (informal)	minus (informal)
one major advantage is . . .	a serious drawback is . . .

> ***One negative aspect*** *of homeworking can be the loss of regular contact with colleagues.*
>
> ***A significant benefit*** *of working from home is the saving of time by not commuting.*

■ Fill the gaps in the following paragraph using language from the table on p. 89.

Every year, millions of students choose to study in a foreign country. This can have considerable (a) _____, such as the chance to experience another culture, but also involves certain (b) _____, which may include feelings of isolation or homesickness. Another (c) _____ aspect may be the high cost, involving both fees and living expenses. However, most students appear to find that the (d) _____ outweigh the (e) _____, and that the chance to join an international group of students is a major (f) _____ in developing a career.

---

2 Organisation

The discussion section can be organised in two ways: either by grouping the benefits and disadvantages together, or by examining the subject from different viewpoints. For example, the following essay title can be discussed in the two ways as shown:

> '*Environmental considerations have no place in a company's strategy – discuss.*'

(a) Grouping all the drawbacks together in one or more paragraphs, then treating the benefits in the same way:

Drawbacks: May increase costs (e.g. 'green' electricity)/delay projects/extra work for managers

---

Benefits: May save money (e.g. reduced packaging)/good PR = increased sales/employee job satisfaction may also be increased

---

Discussion: Depends on nature of business/some costs will rise, others fall/important long-term benefits as consumers place more weight on 'green' considerations

---

(b) Examining the subject from different viewpoints (e.g. economic, ethical or social):

Economic: Initial investment in energy-saving measures may increase costs but long-term benefits should follow
Ethical: Responsible companies should play a part in combating climate change
Social: Consumer-facing companies benefit from 'green' credentials = increased sales/employee job satisfaction may also be increased
Discussion: Depends on nature of business/some costs will rise, others fall/important long-term benefits as consumers place more weight on 'green' considerations

3 Practice A

You have to write an essay titled:

'Discuss whether some employees should be permitted to work from home.'

■ Brainstorm the positive and negative aspects in the box below, and then write an outline using one of the structures (a or b) above.

+	−

Discuss whether some employees should be permitted to work from home.

Outline

(a)

(b)

(c)

(d)

4 Language of discussion

Avoid personal phrases such as *in my opinion* or *personally, I think* . . .

Use impersonal phrases instead such as:

It is generally accepted that	working from home saves commuting time . . .
It is widely agreed that	email and the internet reduce reliance on an office . . .
Most people appear	to need face-to-face contact with colleagues . . .
It is probable that	more companies will encourage working from home . . .
The evidence suggests that	certain people are better at self-management . . .

Certain phrases suggest a minority viewpoint:

| It can be argued that | homeworking encourages time-wasting |
| Some people believe that | homeworkers become isolated |

When you are supporting your opinions with sources, use phrases such as:

| According to Emerson (2011) | few companies have developed clear policies . . . |

5 Counterarguments

In a discussion, you must show that you are familiar with both sides of the argument, and provide reasons to support your position. It is usual to deal with the counterarguments first, before giving your view.

■   **Study the example opposite, and write two more sentences using ideas from the title in section 3.**

Counterargument	Your position
Some people believe that homeworkers become isolated,	but this can be avoided by holding weekly meetings for all departmental staff.

6 Providing evidence

Normally your conclusions on a topic follow an assessment of the evidence. You must show that you have studied the relevant sources, since only then can you give a balanced judgement.

■ Study the following paragraph, which discusses the value of imports to an economy.

THE IMPORTANCE OF IMPORTS

It has frequently been argued that economies benefit from exports, while imports are a regrettable necessity. According to Inglehart (1994), for instance, import controls play an essential role in preventing the unsupportable growth of trade deficits. Governments regularly support export-orientated industries in the belief that their success can strengthen the economy. However, a different view is put forward by Goldberg *et al.* (2009). Their study of the experience of India after it was forced to reduce import tariffs by the IMF in 1991 demonstrates that this led to substantial economic benefits. By permitting capital goods to be imported more cheaply, existing production could be achieved at lower cost, while there was also a growth in the range of new products. Overall, manufacturing output increased by 25% in the six years after 1991. It appears that the traditional economic bias against imports may well be unfounded.

■ Complete the diagram of the paragraph's structure using the following descriptors:

- Writer's viewpoint

- Benefits of imports – Indian case study (Goldberg *et al.*)

- Drawbacks of imports – Inglehart

1	
2	
3	

7 Practice B

■ Write a paragraph on the topic:

'Inflation can be a positive force in the economy – discuss.'

Use the ideas below and give your viewpoint.

Pros:	Encourages spending as people expect higher prices in future Reduces the value of debt The opposite, deflation, causes stagnation (Source: Costa *et al.*, 2012)
Cons:	Workers demand large pay rises, leads to conflict Excessive inflation leads to loss of faith in money Creates uncertainty about future (Source: Patterson, 1998)

▶ See Unit 2.10 Problems and Solutions

UNIT 2.2 Cause and Effect

Academic work frequently involves demonstrating a link between a cause, such as a price rise, and an effect or result, such as a fall in demand. This unit demonstrates and practises two methods of describing the link, with the focus either on the cause or on the effect.

1 The language of cause and effect

A writer may choose to put the emphasis on either the cause or the effect. In both cases, either a verb or a conjunction can be used to show the link.

(a) Focus on causes

With verbs		
The recession	caused created led to resulted in produced	high unemployment
With conjunctions		
Because of Due to Owing to As a result of	**the recession**	there was high unemployment

(b) Focus on effects

With verbs		
High unemployment	*was caused by* *was produced by* *resulted from* (note use of passives)	*the recession*
With conjunctions		
There was **high unemployment**	*due to* *because of* *as a result of*	*the recession*

■ **Compare the following:**

Because prices were cut, sales rose.	(because + verb)
Because of the price cuts, sales rose.	(because of + noun)
As/since prices were cut, sales rose.	(conjunction + verb)
Owing to/due to the price cuts, sales rose.	(conjunction + noun)

Conjunctions are commonly used with specific situations, while verbs are more often used in general cases:

Printing money commonly **leads to** *inflation.*	(general)
Due to *July's hot weather, demand for* *ice cream increased.*	(specific)

Note the position of the conjunctions in the following:

The teacher was ill, **therefore/so/consequently** *the class was cancelled.*

▶ **See Unit 3.5 Conjunctions**

2 Practice A

■ Match the causes with their likely effects and write sentences linking them together.

Causes	Effects
Cold winter of 2013	Increase in labour disputes
Tax cuts	Redundancies
More people shopping on internet	Higher levels of spending
Introduction of digital cameras	Higher levels of saving
Increase in interest rates last spring	**Increased demand for electricity**
Falling sales of a firm's products	Reduced demand for photographic film
Her aggressive managerial style	Stores closing on high street

(a) *Owing to the cold winter of 2013, there was increased demand for electricity.*

(b) _____

_____

(c) _____

_____

(d) _____

_____

(e) _____

_____

(f) _____

_____

(g) _____

_____

3 Practice B

■ **Complete the following sentences with likely effects.**

(a) An increase in the tax on tobacco _____.

(b) Rising demand for MBA courses _____.

(c) Lower fuel prices _____.

(d) Bad weather in the Brazilian coffee-growing region _____.

■ **Complete these sentences with possible causes.**

(e) The company's bankruptcy _____.

(f) The drop in share prices _____ _____.

(g) Hiring extra staff _____.

(h) A significant rise in profits _____.

4 Practice C

■ **Use conjunctions or verbs to complete the following paragraph.**

Unhappy workers

In recent years there appears to have been a growth in employee dissatisfaction with work. At its most extreme this is shown by high rates of suicide in some companies, apparently (a) _____ the stress (b) _____ re-structuring programmes. Surveys of both European and American employees have found that more than 50% were unhappy, often (c) _____ a feeling of stagnation. Various theories have attempted to explain this situation. Employees in certain industries such as car production may feel stressed (d) _____ industry-wide overcapacity, creating a sense of insecurity. More generally, recession can (e) _____ fear of unemployment or short-time working. In addition, the constant drive to cut costs and increase productivity (f) _____ a concern with meeting targets which takes its toll on the workforce. Furthermore, many younger employees are now hired on short-term contracts, which (g) _____ an awareness that they could lose their jobs with little warning.

5 Practice D

■ Study the flow chart below, which shows some of the possible effects of a higher oil price. Complete the paragraph describing this situation.

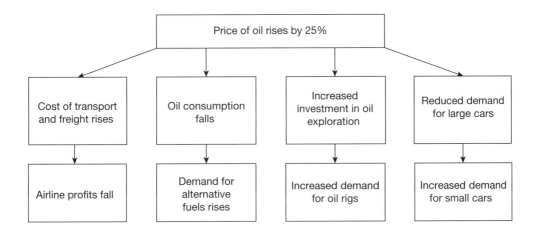

An increase of 25% in the price of oil would have numerous results.
First, it would lead to ...

6 Practice E

■ Choose one of the following situations. Draw a flow chart similar to the one above showing some probable effects, and write a paragraph to describe them.

(a) A property price bubble.

(b) Interest rates reduced below 1% by the central bank.

UNIT 2.3 Cohesion

Cohesion means joining a text together with reference words (e.g. he, theirs) and conjunctions so that the whole text is clear and readable. This unit practises the use of reference words, while conjunctions are examined in Unit 3.5.

1 Reference words

These are used to avoid repetition:

John Maynard Keynes (1883–1946) was an influential British economist whose theories had a profound effect on economic thought during the 1930s and later. **He** argued that governments should spend money to stimulate the economy, even if **they** had to borrow to do so. **This** 'deficit spending' was the basis of the New Deal in the USA, which allowed **it** to overcome the Great Depression of 1929–1933. Keynes' theories became unfashionable in the 1970s, but **they** were revived following the recession of 2007–2009.

Here, the reference words function as follows:

Keynes	governments	spend money	USA	theories
He	they	This	it	they

■ Study these examples of reference words and phrases.

Pronouns	he/she/it/they
Possessive pronouns	his/her/hers/its/their/theirs
Objective pronouns	her/him/them
Demonstrative pronouns	this/that/these/those
Other phrases	the former/the latter/the first/the second/the last

2 Practice A

■ Read the following paragraph and complete the table.

BUSINESS SHORT LIFE

La Ferrera (2007) has researched the life cycle of new businesses. She found that they have an average life of only 4.7 years, and considers this is due to two main reasons; one economic and one social. The former appears to be a lack of capital, the latter a failure to carry out sufficient market research. La Ferrera considers that together these account for approximately 70% of business failures.

Reference	Reference word/phrase
La Ferrera	*She*
new businesses	
average life of only 4.7 years	
one economic	
one social	
the former . . ., the latter . . .	

3 Preventing confusion

To avoid confusing the reader, it is important to use reference words only when the reference is clear. For example:

> *The company was founded in 1953 and bought the mine in 1957. It was successful at first* . . .

In this case, it is not clear which noun (the company or the mine) 'It' refers to. So to avoid this, write:

> *The company was founded in 1953 and bought the mine in 1957. The mine/the latter was successful at first* . . .

4 Practice B

■   Read the text below and replace the words in bold with reference words.

VELCRO

Velcro is a fabric fastener used with clothes and shoes. **Velcro** was invented by a Swiss engineer called George de Mestral. **Mestral's** idea was derived from studying the tiny hooks found on some plant seeds. **The tiny hooks** cling to animals and help disperse the seeds. Velcro has two sides, one of which is covered in small hooks and the other in loops. When **the hooks and loops** are pressed together they form a strong bond.

Mestral spent eight years perfecting **Mestral's** invention, which **Mestral** called 'Velcro' from the French words 'velour' and 'crochet'. **The invention** was patented in 1955 and today over 60 million metres of Velcro are sold annually.

---

5 Practice C

■ In the following paragraph, insert suitable reference words in the gaps.

Gillette's blades

Thin, disposable razor blades were marketed in America by King Gillette at the beginning of the twentieth century. (a) _____ had realised that as all men had to shave daily, there was a huge market for a product that would make (b) _____ easier. (c) _____ was a simple idea, but at first (d) _____ found it very hard to sell (e) _____.
(f) _____ was because nobody had marketed a throw-away product before. However, (g) _____ use of advertising to stimulate demand rapidly increased sales and (h) _____ became very popular. Within a few years (i) _____ was a millionaire.

---

6 Practice D

■ Use the following information to write a paragraph about nylon, paying careful attention to the use of reference words.

Nylon

Inventor: Wallace Carothers

Company: DuPont Corporation (USA)

Carothers' position: Director of research centre

Carothers' background: Chemistry student, specialising in polymers (molecules composed of long chains of atoms)

Properties: Strong but fine synthetic fibre

Patented: 1935

Mass produced: 1939

Applications: Stockings, toothbrushes, parachutes, fishing lines, surgical thread

UNIT
2.4

Comparisons

It is often necessary to make comparisons in academic writing. The comparison might be the subject of the essay, or might be given just to provide evidence for the argument. In all cases, it is important to explain clearly what is being compared and to make the comparison as accurate as possible. This chapter illustrates various forms of comparison and practises their use.

1 Comparison structures

Some studies are based on a comparison:

The purpose of this study is to compare Chinese and American consumers on their propensity to use self-service technology in a retail setting . . .

In other cases, a comparison provides useful context:

China's GDP in 2008 was $4.4 trillion, smaller than Japan's and less than a third of America's.

The two basic comparative forms are:

(a) *France's economy is **larger** than Holland's.*

*The students were **happier** after the exam.*

(-er is added to one-syllable adjectives and two-syllable adjectives ending in -y, which changes into an 'i')

(b) *The Vietnamese economy is **more dynamic** than Argentina's.*

(more . . . is used with other adjectives of two or more syllables)

These comparisons can be modified by the use of adverbs such as *slightly, considerably, significantly* and *substantially*:

> *The Dutch economy is **slightly larger** than Australia's.*

> *Russia's GDP is **substantially smaller** than Mexico's.*

Similarity can be noted by the use of *as . . . as*:

> *France's population is **as large as** Britain's.*

This form can also be used for quantitative comparison:

> *Britain is half **as large as** France.* (also *twice as large as, ten times as fast as*)

▶   **See Unit 3.6 Numbers**

2 Practice A

■   **Study the table, which shows the price of quality residential property in various cities. Complete the comparisons, and write two more.**

€ per m²	City
28,000	London
16,500	New York
16,200	Moscow
16,000	Paris
15,850	Tokyo
13,500	Rome
11,850	Singapore
11,000	Sydney

(a) Residential property in London is twice as expensive _____ in Rome.

(b) Property in Moscow is _____ cheaper than in New York.

(c) Tokyo property is nearly as expensive as property in _____.

(d) Singapore has significantly cheaper property _____ New York.

(e) London is the _____ expensive of the eight cities, while Sydney is the cheapest.

(f) _____.

(g) _____.

3 Forms of comparison

Compare these three structures:

> *Parisian property is more expensive than Roman (property).*
>
> *Property in Paris is more expensive than in Rome.*
>
> *The price of property in Paris is higher than in Rome.*

Note that high/low are used for comparing abstract ideas (e.g. rates of inflation):

> *Unemployment is **lower** in the cities than the country.*

More/less must be used with *than + comparison*:

> *Current inflation is **less than** last year's rate.*

4 Using superlatives

When using superlatives, take care to define the group (e.g. 'the cheapest car' has no meaning)

> *The cheapest car **in the Ford range/in the USA**.*

The most/the least are followed by an adjective:

> *The **most interesting** example is Ireland* . . .

The most/the fewest are used in relation to numbers:

> ***The fewest** students studied insurance* . . . (i.e. the lowest number)

5 Practice B

■ Study the table, which shows the income of the top ten clubs in European football. Then read the comparisons. Each sentence contains one error. Find and correct it.

Income of leading European football clubs 2012–2013

Club	Revenue (€ million)
Real Madrid	518
FC Barcelona	482
Bayern Munich	431
Manchester United	423
Paris Saint Germain	398
Manchester City	316
Chelsea	303
Arsenal	284
Juventus	272
AC Milan	263

(a) Real Madrid was the richest football club.

(b) Real Madrid's income was almost twice much as AC Milan's.

(c) FC Barcelona earned marginally more than Manchester City.

(d) Juventus had less revenue Arsenal.

(e) Chelsea's income was slightly lower than Bayern Munich's.

(f) Manchester United earned approximately same as Bayern Munich.

6 Practice C

■ The table shows the percentage of GDP spent on health in a range of countries. Complete the gaps in the following paragraph (one word each).

Country	Health spending as % of GDP
USA	14
Switzerland	11
Canada	9.5
South Africa	8.6
Denmark	8.4
Bangladesh	3.5
Oman	3.0
Indonesia	2.4
Madagascar	2.0
Azerbaijan	0.9

There are wide (a) _____ in the percentage of GDP spent on health by different countries. The USA spends 14% of GDP, (b) _____ times as much as Bangladesh, and over five times (c) _____ much as Indonesia. South Africa (8.6%) spends (d) _____ more (e) _____ Denmark. At the lower end, Madagascar only spends 2%, which is (f) _____ as much as Azerbaijan.

7 Practice D

■ The table below gives some data on two major British supermarket chains, Sainsbury's and Morrisons. Write a paragraph comparing them.

	Annual turnover £m.	Profits before tax £m.	Employees	Market share	Number of supermarkets	Number of convenience stores
Sainsbury's	26,353	898	157,000	16.8%	592	611
Morrisons	17,680	−176	130,000	12.2%	500	80

UNIT 2.5 **Definite Articles**

Students often find the rules for using articles ('a', 'an' and 'the') in English confusing. This chapter focuses on the definite article, 'the', and provides guidelines, examples and practice.

1 Using articles

Unless they are uncountable, all nouns need an article when used in the singular. The article can be either **a/an** or **the**. Compare:

(a) *The Central Bank has reduced the cost of borrowing again.*

(b) *She went to a bank to change some dollars.*

In (a), a specific bank is identified.

In (b), the name of the bank is not important.

▶ **See Unit 2.12 Singular or Plural?**

2 Definite articles

The rules for using **the** (the definite article) are quite complex.

■ **Decide why it is used, or not used, in the following examples.**

(a) The world's largest motor manufacturer by revenue is Volkswagen.

(b) The USA was founded in the eighteenth century.

(c) The government increased regulation of banks in the 1930s.

(d) In many companies, the knowledge of most employees is a wasted resource.

(e) *The Economist* is published every week.

(f) The south is characterised by poverty and emigration.

(g) John Maynard Keynes, the British economist, died in 1946.

(h) The River Seine runs through the middle of Paris.

(i) The World Bank was founded in 1945.

(j) The euro was introduced in 2002.

3 Guidelines

In general, **the** is used with:

(a) superlatives (*largest*)

(b) time periods (*eighteenth century/1930s*)

(c) unique things (government, world)

(d) specified things (*knowledge of most employees*)

(e) regular publications (*Economist*)

(f) regions and rivers (*south/River Seine*)

(g) very well-known people and things (*British economist*)

(h) institutions and bodies (*World Bank*)

(i) positions (*middle*)

(j) currencies (*euro*)

It is **not** used with:

(k) things in general (*banks*)

(l) names of countries, except for the UK, the USA and a few others

(m) abstract nouns (e.g. *inflation*)

(n) companies/things named after people/places (e.g. *Sainsbury's, Heathrow Airport*)

4 Practice A

Students often have difficulty deciding if a noun phrase is specific or not. Compare:

Climate change is a serious threat for many countries. (not specific)

The Russian climate is characterised by long cold winters. (specific)

■ In the following sentences, decide if the words and phrases in bold are specific or not, and whether 'the' should be added.

Example:

_____ **inflation** was a serious concern for _____ **Brazilian government**.
Inflation was a serious concern for **the** Brazilian government.

(a) _____ **electrical engineering** is the main industry in _____ **northern region**.

(b) _____ **energy firms** have made record profits in _____ **financial year 2012–2013**.

(c) _____ **global warming** is partly caused by _____ **fossil fuels**.

(d) _____**company's CEO** has been arrested on _____ **fraud charges**.

(e) _____ **theft** is costing _____ **banking business** millions of dollars a year.

(f) _____ **tourism** is _____ **world's** biggest industry.

(g) _____ **forests of Scandinavia** produce most of _____ **Britain's paper**.

(h) _____ **Thai currency** is _____ **baht**.

(i) _____ **computer crime** has grown by 200% in _____ **last decade**.

(j) _____ **main causes** of _____ **Industrial Revolution** are still debated.

(k) Already 3% of _____ **working population** are employed in _____ **call centres**.

(l) _____ **latest forecast** predicts _____ **rising unemployment** for two years.

(m) Research on _____ **housing market** is being conducted in _____ **business school**.

(n) _____ **best definition** is often _____ **simplest**.

5 Practice B

■ Complete the following text by inserting a/an/the (or nothing) in each gap. (Note that in some cases, more than one answer is possible.)

Microfinance is (a) _____ name given to a system of lending money to

poor people in (b) _____ developing countries. Pioneered by Mohammad

Yunus of (c) _____ Grameen Bank in (d) _____ Bangladesh,

it has been claimed that this process allows 5% of the customers to leave

(e) _____ poverty every year, while almost all the clients pay

back (f) _____ loans on time. It is, however, quite difficult to

research (g) _____ effectiveness of microcredit, because of

(h) _____ difficulty of organising a study. Simply comparing borrowers

with non-borrowers is unhelpful, since non-borrowers are likely to be less

entrepreneurial. But a recent study by (i) _____ two researchers from

MIT, (j) _____ American university, in (k) _____ Indian city of

Hyderabad, which compared two similar city slums, one with microcredit available

and one without, found that (l) _____ process had little significant

benefit, with only 20% of loans leading to (m) _____ creation of

(n) _____ new businesses.

UNIT
2.6

Definitions

Definitions are usually found in introductions (see Unit 1.10 Introductions and Conclusions). They are not needed in every case, but if the title includes an unfamiliar phrase, or if the writer wants to use a term in a special way, it is worth making clear to the reader exactly what is meant in this context. This unit presents ways of writing both simple and complex definitions.

1 Simple definitions

Basic definitions are formed by giving a category and the application:

Word	Category	Application
An agenda	is a set of issues	to be discussed in a meeting.
A Master's degree	is an academic award	for postgraduate students, given on successful completion of a dissertation.
A grant	is a sum of money	given for a specific purpose.

■ Complete the following definitions by inserting a suitable category word from the box.

---

organisation   period   financial instrument   loan   agreement   costs

---

(a) A mortgage is a type of _____ used for buying property in which the lender has the security of the property.

(b) A multinational company is a business _____ that operates in various countries.

(c) A recession is a _____ of negative economic growth.

(d) A cartel is an _____ between a group of companies for the purpose of price-fixing.

(e) Overheads are the fixed _____ of a business, not related to production.

(f) A bond is a _____ offering a fixed rate of return over a limited period.

■ Write definitions for the following:

(g) A trades union _____.

(h) A monopoly _____.

(i) Marketing _____.

(j) A dividend _____.

(k) A hostile takeover _____.

2 Complex definitions

The following examples illustrate the variety of methods that can be used in giving definitions.

■ Study the examples and underline the term being defined.

(a) The definition for a failed project ranges from abandoned projects to projects that do not meet their full potential or simply have schedule overrun problems.

(b) Development is a socio-economic-technological process having the main objective of raising the standard of living of the people.

(c) Electronic commerce is characterised by an absence of physical proximity between the buyer and seller in conducting the search, assessment and transaction stages of a transaction.

(d) Corporate governance is a set of mechanisms, both institutional and market-based, designed to mitigate agency problems that arise from the separation of ownership and control in a company.

(e) Globalisation, in an economic sense, describes the opening up of national economies to global markets and global capital, the freer movement and diffusion of goods, services, finance, people, knowledge and technology around the world.

(f) Empathy as a concept has an interesting history. As Eisenberg and Strayer (1987) note: 'Some people take the term empathy to refer to a cognitive process analogous to cognitive role taking (e.g. Deutsch and Madle, 1975); others take it to mean . . .'.

■ **Working with a partner, decide which example(s):**

(i)   gives a variety of relevant situations

(ii) defines the term in a negative way

(iii) quotes a definition from another writer

(iv) uses category words

(v)   explains a process

3 Practice

When writing introductions, it is often useful to define a term in the title, even if it is fairly common, in order to demonstrate your understanding of its meaning.

■ **Study the following titles, underline the terms that are worth defining, and write a definition for three of them.**

(a) Do 'managing diversity' policies and practices in Human Resource Management add value?

(b) How can the management of an entrepreneurial business retain its entrepreneurial culture as it matures?

(c) Why is organisational culture of sustained interest not only for academics, but also for practising managers?

(d) Is it true that firms in perfect competition do not make a profit?

■ **Think of a topic you are currently studying and write a definition for a term used in that topic that needs clarification.**

UNIT
2.7

Examples

Examples are used in academic writing for support and illustration. Suitable examples can strengthen the argument, but they can also help the reader to understand a point. This unit demonstrates the different ways in which examples can be introduced, and practises their use.

1 Using examples

Generalisations are commonly used to introduce a topic:

> *It is often claimed that many mergers are unsuccessful . . .*

But if the reader is given an example for illustration, the idea becomes more concrete:

> *It is often claimed that many mergers are unsuccessful, for instance the merger between Compaq and Hewlett-Packard in 2005 . . .*

Without examples, an argument may seem too theoretical:

> *E-commerce businesses are particularly vulnerable to security breaches.*

An example makes the idea easier to understand:

> *E-commerce businesses are particularly vulnerable to security breaches. When eBay was hacked into in 2014, for instance, 128 million members had to change their passwords.*

The example may also support the point the writer is making:

> *. . . in recent years researchers have begun looking into corporate governance in transition economies . . . For example, Djankov and Murrell (2002) document that more than 150,000 large SOEs in transition economies have undergone enterprise restructuring . . .*

■   Decide which of the following use examples for support and which for illustration.

(a) The use of incentive compensation, such as bonus and stock options, is an important means of motivating and compensating executives of private companies, especially executives of technology-orientated companies.

(b) Earlier studies have also documented that the cost of holding an under-diversified portfolio can be substantial. For example, Peters (1991) shows how differential diversification abilities of managers . . .

(c) Other consumers, however, intentionally avoid such self-service technologies. For example, some retailers who are using in-store internet kiosks have found that not all consumers are interested in using the new technology (Mearin, 2001).

▶   See Unit 2.8 Generalisations

2 Phrases to introduce examples

(a) **for instance**, **for example** (with commas)

Some car manufacturers, for instance Hyundai, now offer five-year guarantees . . .

(b) **such as, e.g.**

Many entrepreneurs, such as Richard Branson, have no formal business qualifications . . .

(c) **particularly, especially** (to give a focus)

Certain MBA courses, especially American ones, take two years . . .

(d) **a case in point** (for single examples)

A few countries have experienced deflation. A case in point is Japan . . .

■   Add a suitable example to each sentence below and introduce it with a phrase from the box above.

Example: Certain industries are experiencing labour shortages.

*Certain industries, **for instance engineering**, are experiencing labour shortages.*

(a) Some twentieth-century inventions affected the lives of most people.

(b) A number of sports have become very profitable due to the sale of television rights.

(c) Various companies have built their reputation on the strength of one product.

(d) Some brands have remained successful for more than 50 years.

(e) In recent years, the product life cycle has tended to get shorter.

(f) A variety of products are promoted by celebrity endorsement.

(g) Speculation in some commodities has created price bubbles.

(h) Investors are often advised to spread their risk by putting their money into a range of investments.

3 Practice A

■ Study the following text and add examples from the box where suitable, using an introductory phrase from section 2 on p. 117.

---

free delivery or discounted prices   bookshops

clothing and footwear   books and music

many supermarkets offer delivery services for online customers

---

THE CHANGING FACE OF SHOPPING

Widespread use of the internet has led to a major change in shopping habits. It is no longer necessary to visit shops to make routine purchases. With more specialised items, internet retailers can offer a wider range of products than bricks-and-mortar shops. They can also provide extra incentives to customers, in addition to the convenience of not having to visit a real shop. As a result, certain types of store are disappearing from the high street. Other products, however, appear to require personal inspection and approval, and in addition many people enjoy the activity of shopping, so it seems unlikely that the internet will completely replace the shopping centre.

4 Practice B

■ Read the text opposite and then insert suitable examples where needed to illustrate the points.

A NEW PERSPECTIVE?

Students who go to study abroad often experience a type of culture shock when they arrive in the new country. Customs which they took for granted in their own society may not be followed in the host country. Even everyday patterns of life may be different. When these are added to the inevitable differences which occur in every country students may at first feel confused. They may experience rapid changes of mood, or even want to return home. However, most soon make new friends and, in a relatively short period, are able to adjust to their new environment. They may even find that they prefer some aspects of their new surroundings, and forget that they are not at home for a while!

5 Restatement

Another small group of phrases is used when there is only one 'example'. This is a kind of restatement:

The world's leading gold producer (i.e. South Africa) has been faced with a number of technical difficulties.

in other words	namely	that is (to say)	i.e.	viz. (very formal)

■ **Add a suitable phrase from the box below to the following sentences to make them clearer.**

(a) The company's overheads doubled last year.

(b) During a bear market, few investors make money.

(c) The Indian capital has a thriving commercial centre.

(d) The best-selling car of all time has ceased production.

i.e. the Toyota Cotolla
in other words the fixed costs
that is a period of falling share prices
namely New Delhi

UNIT
2.8

Generalisations

Generalisations are often used to introduce a topic. They can be powerful statements because they are simple and easy to understand, but they must be used with care, to avoid being overly simplistic or inaccurate. This unit explains how to generalise clearly and effectively.

1 Using generalisations

Generalisations are used to give a basic picture of a topic. Compare:

54.9% of Spanish companies employ fewer than ten people.

The majority of Spanish companies employ fewer than ten people.

Although the first sentence is more accurate, the second is easier to understand and remember. The writer must decide when accuracy is necessary, and when a generalisation will be acceptable. For example, the graph below shows the London stock market's performance during one day:

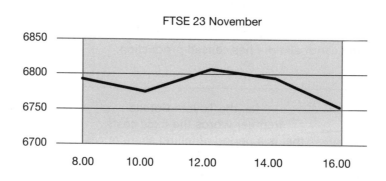

For most purposes, it is adequate to generalise the performance as:

The FTSE 100 index fell 40 points on 23 November.

This ignores the hour-by-hour changes but gives an overall picture.

2 Structure

Generalisations can be made in two ways:

(a) Most commonly using the plural:

      Joint stock companies began in the sixteenth century.

(b) Using the singular + definite article (more formal):

      The joint stock company began in the sixteenth century.

      Avoid absolute phrases in generalisations such as:

      Small companies adapt faster to changing markets.

      Instead, it is better to use cautious phrases such as:

      Small companies tend to adapt faster to changing markets.

▶ **See Unit 2.13 Style (6 Caution)**

■ **Write generalisations on the following topics.**

(a) market research/new products

      Example: Market research can be vital for evaluating new products.

(b) job satisfaction/rate of pay

_____

(c) weak currency/level of exports

_____

(d) spending on R&D/introduction of new products

_____

(e) unemployment/level of consumer spending

_____

(f) cold weather/demand for gas

_____

3 Overgeneralising

This means making statements that are too simple or inaccurate. For example, using income figures from the table below, a writer might claim:

People were much richer in 2009 than 20 years earlier.

But this ignores inflation over the period. It is more accurate to say:

Average incomes doubled between 1989 and 2009.

Comparison of some key UK economic indicators, 1989–2009

Britain	1989	1999	2009
Inflation rate	7.8%	3.4%	1.9%
Interest rate	13.7%	5.5%	0.5%
Unemployment	6.1%	4.6%	7.8%
Average income	£11,700	£19,000	£24,000
Average house price	£61,500	£68,300	£160,000

■ Some of the following sentences are accurate, but others are overgeneralised. Rewrite the latter more accurately.

(a) The average price of houses more than doubled between 1999 and 2009.

(b) During the two decades 1989–2009, unemployment remained below 10%.

(c) 2009 was the worst year for savers.

(d) In relation to income, houses were cheaper in 1999 than 2009.

4 Practice

■ Read the following text and write five generalisations about encouraging entrepreneurship.

ENCOURAGING ENTREPRENEURSHIP

Many countries have attempted to copy the example of Silicon Valley in California and tried to create their own entrepreneurial centres of new technology. However, these attempts are rarely successful, partly because they ignore the reasons why the original was so outstanding: being close to two first-class universities and a major financial centre.

Three patterns for developing entrepreneurial powerhouses have been identified. The first is where a major company stimulates the growth of surrounding smaller firms. Another can occur when a recession creates widespread redundancy among skilled workers, who use their knowledge to create a cluster of new businesses. Finally, a successful local businessman or woman may build an enterprise that creates opportunities for others.

But two other ingredients can affect results: chance and culture. If the culture is filled with barriers to business development, the more enterprising are likely to take their ideas somewhere more suitable, as many Indians did in the 1960s and 70s.

(a) _____

(b) _____

(c) _____

(d) _____

(e) _____

5 Building on generalisations

Most essays move from the general to the specific, as a generalisation has to be supported and developed. For example, an essay with the title 'The impact of globalisation on the Chinese economy' might develop in this way:

Generalisation	Support	Development > Specific
Since the mid-twentieth century, there has been a remarkable increase in international trade.	The reasons for this are a combination of international agreements such as GATT, better transport and improved communications.	China has played a significant part in the process, with its international trade growing by 16 times in just 20 years, while its GDP increased by nearly 10% per year.

■ Choose a title from the list below, write a generalisation, and then support and develop it in the same way.

(a) People are often positively disposed to their own country's products – discuss.

(b) To what extent has management theory made space for gender?

(c) Evaluate the contribution of Small and Medium Enterprises (SMEs) to the economy.

(d) Compare and contrast the challenges facing big business groups in China, Japan and South Korea.

▶ See Unit 1.10 Introductions and Conclusions

Passives

The passive form is a feature of much academic writing, making it more impersonal and formal, but the passive should not be overused. This chapter provides practice in developing a balanced style.

1 Active and passive

■ Compare these two sentences:

The company *was founded in 1925 by Walter Trimble.* (passive)

Walter Trimble *founded the company in 1925.* (active)

In the first sentence, the emphasis is on the company, in the second on Trimble. The passive is used when the writer wants to focus on the result, not on the cause. So the passive is often used in written English when the cause (a person or thing) is less important or unknown.

*Aluminium **was first produced** in the nineteenth century.* (by someone)

*The currency **was devalued** in the 1930s.* (due to something)

The cause of the action can be shown by adding 'by . . .':

*The banking crisis **was caused** by excessive speculation.*

The passive is also used in written work to provide a more impersonal style:

*The findings **were evaluated**.* (not 'I evaluated the findings')

▶ See Unit 2.13 Style

2 Structure

All passive structures have two parts:

Form of the verb to be	Past participle
is	constructed
was	developed
will be	reorganised

■ Change the following into the passive.

(a) We collected the data and compared the two groups.

(b) I interviewed 120 people from six similar businesses.

(c) They checked the results and found several errors.

(d) We will make an analysis of the findings.

(e) He asked four managers to give their opinions.

(f) She wrote the report and distributed ten copies.

3 Using adverbs

An adverb can be inserted into a passive form to add information:

*This process is **commonly** called 'networking'.*

■ Change the following sentences from active to passive and insert a suitable adverb from the box below. Decide if it is necessary to show a cause.

optimistically	helpfully	effectively	accurately
eventually	carefully	profitably	vigorously

Example: The recession forced half the companies to make redundancies.

*Half the companies were **eventually** forced to make redundancies by the recession.*

(a) The Connors family ran the company until 2001.

(b) Economists debated the reasons for the Asian currency crisis.

(c) They provided pencils for all students in the exam.

(d) The staff of the advertising agency gave a presentation.

(e) The researchers calculated the percentages to three decimal places.

(f) They called their business the Grand Universal Trading Company.

(g) She researched the life cycles of over 240 companies.

4 Practice A

In most texts, the active and the passive are mixed.

■ **Read the following text and underline the passive forms.**

BOOTS THE CHEMISTS

When John Boot died at 45, he was worn out by the effort of establishing his herbal medicine business. He had spent his early years as a farm labourer but had worked his way up to be the owner of a substantial business. He was born in 1815, became a member of a Methodist chapel in Nottingham, and later moved to the city. John was concerned by the situation of the poor, who could not afford a doctor, and in 1849 he opened a herbal medicine shop which was called the British and American Botanic Establishment. In the early stages John was helped financially by his father in law, while his mother provided herbal knowledge.

On his death in 1860 the business was taken over by his wife, and she was soon assisted by their 10-year-old son, Jesse. He quickly showed the business ability which transformed his father's shop into a national business. Jesse opened more shops in poor districts of the city and pioneered advertising methods. He also insisted on doing business in cash, rather than offering his customers credit.

5 Practice B

■ **List the passives in the table opposite. Decide if the active could be used instead, and rewrite it if so.**

Passive	Active possible?	Active
He was worn out	Yes	The effort ...had worn him out

■ What would be the effect of using the passive throughout the text?

6 Practice C

The passive is used more in written than in spoken English, but should not be overused, as it can give a very formal tone.

■ In the following text, which continues the history of the Boots company, passives are used throughout. Change some of them into the active.

In 1889, he was introduced to Florence Rowe, the daughter of a bookseller, while on holiday. After they were married the business was affected by her ideas: the product range was enlarged to include stationery and books. The Boots subscription library and in-store cafes were also introduced due to Florence's influence. During World War I the Boots factories were used to make a variety of products, from sterilisers to gas masks. But after the war Jesse was attacked by arthritis and, worried by the economic prospects, the company was sold to an American rival for £2 m. This, however, was made bankrupt during the Depression and Boots was then bought by a British group for £6 m, and Jesse's son, John, was made chairman. The famous No. 7 cosmetics range was launched in the 1930s and in World War II both saccharin and penicillin were produced in the factories. However, recently the company has been threatened by intense competition from supermarkets in its core pharmaceutical business.

UNIT 2.10 Problems and Solutions

> Writing tasks frequently ask students to examine a problem and evaluate a range of solutions. This unit explains ways in which this kind of text can be organised. Note that some of the language is similar to that practised in Unit 2.1 Argument and Discussion.

1 Paragraph structure

■ Study the organisation of the following paragraph:

HOW CAN ROAD CONGESTION BE REDUCED?

Currently, roads are often congested, which is expensive in terms of delays to the movement of people and freight. It is commonly suggested that building more roads, or widening existing ones, would ease the traffic jams. But not only is the cost of such work high, but the construction process adds to the congestion, while the resulting extra road space may encourage extra traffic. Therefore constructing more road space is unlikely to solve the problem, and other remedies, such as road pricing or greater use of public transport, should be examined.

(a) Problem	*Currently, roads are often congested, which is expensive in terms of delays to the movement of people and freight.*
(b) Solution A	*It is commonly suggested that building more roads, or widening existing ones, would ease the traffic jams.*
(c) Arguments against solution A	*But not only is the cost of such work high, but the construction process adds to the congestion, while the resulting extra road space may encourage extra traffic.*
(d) Conclusion in favour of solutions B and C	*. . . other remedies, such as road pricing or greater use of public transport, should be examined.*

2 Alternative conclusion

The same ideas could be reordered to arrive at a different conclusion:

HOW CAN ROAD CONGESTION BE REDUCED?

Currently, roads are often congested, which is expensive in terms of delays to the movement of people and freight. It is commonly suggested that building more roads, or widening existing ones, would ease the traffic jams. This remedy is criticised for being expensive and liable to lead to more road use. This may be partly true, yet the alternatives are equally problematic. Road pricing has many practical difficulties, while people are reluctant to use public transport. There is little alternative to a road-building programme except increasing road chaos.

Problem	*Currently, roads are often congested, which is expensive in terms of delays to the movement of people and freight.*
Solution A	*It is commonly suggested that building more roads, or widening existing ones, would ease the traffic jams.*
Arguments against solution A	*This remedy is criticised for being expensive and liable to lead to more road use, which may be partly true . . .*
Solutions B and C and arguments against	*. . . yet the alternatives are equally problematic. Road pricing has many practical difficulties, while people are reluctant to use public transport.*
Conclusion in favour of solution A	*There is little alternative to a road-building programme except increasing road chaos.*

3 Practice A

■ Analyse the following paragraph in a similar way:

MANAGING TOURISM GROWTH

Many developing countries have found that the development of a tourism industry can bring social and environmental drawbacks. Growing visitor numbers can cause pollution and put pressure on scarce resources such as water. One possible solution is to target upmarket holidaymakers, in order to get the maximum profit from minimum numbers. However, this is a limited market and requires considerable investment in infrastructure and training. Another remedy is to rigorously control the environmental standards of any development, in order to minimise the impact of the construction. This requires effective government agencies, but is likely to ensure the best outcome for both tourists and locals.

Problem	
Solution A	
Arguments against solution A	
Solution B	
Conclusion in favour of solution B	

4 Vocabulary

The following words can be used as synonyms for **problem** and **solution**.

*three main **difficulties** have arisen . . .*   *the best **remedy** for this may be . . .*

*the main **challenge** faced by SMEs . . .*   *two **answers** have been put forward . . .*

*one of the **concerns** during the recession . . .*   *another **suggestion** is . . .*

*the new process created two **questions** . . .*   *Matheson's **proposal** was finally accepted.*

*the team faced six **issues** . . .*   *This was **rectified/solved** by . . .*

*our principal **worry/dilemma** was . . .*

5 Practice B

■ Write a paragraph to evaluate solutions to the problem of university expansion using the notes below.

Topic: University expansion

Problem: Demand for university places is growing, leading to overcrowding in lectures and seminars

Solution A: Increase fees to reduce demand

Argument against A: Unfair to poorer students

Solution B: Government pays to expand universities

Argument against B: Unfair to average taxpayers, who would be subsidising the education of a minority who will earn high salaries

Conclusion: Government should subsidise poorer students

6 Practice C

■ Think of a similar problem in your subject area. Complete the table and write a paragraph that leads to a conclusion.

Topic	
Problem	
Solution A	
Argument against A	
Solution B	
Argument against B	
(Solution C)	
Conclusion	

▶   See Unit 2.1 Argument and Discussion

UNIT
2.11 **Punctuation**

> Accurate punctuation and use of capital letters help the reader to understand exactly what the writer meant. While some aspects of punctuation, such as the use of commas, can be a matter of individual style, correct punctuation in areas such as quotation is vital.

1 Capital letters

It is difficult to give precise rules about the use of capital letters in modern English, where there is a trend to use them less. However, they should always be used in the following cases:

(a) The first word in a sentence	*In the beginning . . .*
(b) Names of organisations	*Penn State University*
(c) Days and months	*Friday, 21 July*
(d) Nationality words	*France and the French*
(e) Names of people/places	*Dr Martin Lee from Singapore*
(f) Book titles (main words only)	*Protectionism and Industrial Decline*
(g) Academic subjects	*She studied Economics and Accounting*

2 Apostrophes (')

These are one of the most confusing features of English punctuation. They are mainly used in two situations:

(a) to show contractions   *He's the leading authority on tax reform*

    NB: contractions are not common in academic English

(b) with possessives   *The professor's secretary* (singular)
                                       Students' marks (plural words ending in 's')
                                       Women's rights (for irregular plurals)

    NB: **It's** is the contraction of **it is**   *It's possible the course will be cancelled*

    The possessive form is **its**   *Civilization and its Discontents*

3 Semicolons (;)

They are used to show the link between two connected phrases, when a comma would be too weak and a full stop too strong:

20 people were interviewed for the first study; 33 for the second.

Semicolons are also used to divide up items in a list when they have a complex structure, as in a multiple citation:

(Maitland, 2006; Rosenor, 1997; The Economist, 2006b; University of Michigan, 2000).

4 Colons (:)

Colons are used:

(a) to introduce explanations   *The meeting was postponed: the Dean was ill.*

(b) to start a list   *Three aspects were identified: financial, social and ethical.*

(c) to introduce a quotation   *As the Duchess of Windsor said: 'You can never be too rich or too thin'.*

5 Commas (,)

These are one of the most common punctuation marks, but also the hardest to provide guidance for, since comma use is partly a matter of individual style. It is useful to think of commas as providing a brief pause for readers, to give them a chance to make sense of a chunk of text. Overuse can slow down the reader, but equally a lack of commas can cause confusion.

Some instances of necessary comma usage are:

(a) after introductory words or phrases:

> *However, more cases should be considered before reaching a conclusion.*

(b) around examples or comments:

> *Certain investments, for instance shares, are highly volatile.*

> *Nationalism, it is widely recognised, has a positive and negative side.*

(c) with some conjunctions:

> *Three hundred people were interviewed, but only half the responses could be used.*

(d) in lists:

> *Apostrophes, colons, semicolons and commas must all be used with care.*

6 Quotations marks/inverted commas ("..."/'...')

(a) Single quotation marks are used to emphasise a word:

> *The word 'factory' was first used in the seventeenth century.*

To give quotations from other writers:

> *Goodwin's (1977) analysis of habit indicates that, in general, 'it will be more difficult to reverse a trend than to accentuate it'.*

To show direct speech:

> *'Can anyone find the answer?' asked the lecturer.*

NB: Longer quotations are usually indented (i.e. have a wider margin) and/or are set in smaller type.

(b) Double quotation marks are used to show quotations inside quotations (nested quotations):

> *As Kauffman remarked: 'his concept of "internal space" requires close analysis'.*

(c) In references, quotation marks are used for the names of articles and chapters, but book or journal titles normally use italics:

> Russell, T. (1995) 'A future for coffee?' *Journal of Applied Marketing* 6, 14–17.

▶ **See Unit 1.7 References and Quotations**

7 Full stops (.)

These are used to show the end of a sentence:

> *The first chapter provides a clear introduction to the topic.*

They are also used with certain abbreviations, when these are the first part of a word:

> *govt./Jan./p. 397*

But do not use full stops with abbreviations such as:

> *BBC/UN/VIP*

▶ **See Unit 3.2 Abbreviations**

8 Others

Hyphens (-) are used with certain words, such as compound nouns, and certain structures:

> *A well-researched, thought-provoking book.*
>
> *Her three-year-old daughter is learning to read.*

Exclamation marks (!) and question marks (?):

> *'Well!' he shouted, 'Who would believe it?'*

Brackets or parentheses ( ) can be used to give additional detail:

> *Employee attitudes do not affect other dimensions of customer satisfaction (price and quality).*

9 Practice A

■ **Punctuate the following sentences.**

(a) the study was carried out by christine zhen-wei qiang of the world bank

(b) professor rowans new book the triumph of capitalism is published in new york

(c) as keynes said its better to be roughly right than precisely wrong

(d) three departments law business and economics have had their funding cut

(e) as cammack 1994 points out latin america is creating a new phenomenon democracy without citizens

(f)   thousands of new words such as app enter the english language each year

(g) in 2005 frances per capita gdp was 73% of americas

(h) she scored 56% on the main course the previous semester she had achieved 67%

10 Practice B

■ Punctuate the following text.

the london school of business is offering three new courses this year economics with psychology introduction to management and ecommerce the first is taught by dr jennifer hillary and runs from october to january the second introduction to management for msc finance students is offered in the second semester and is assessed by coursework only professor wangs course in ecommerce runs in both the autumn and the spring and is for more experienced students

Singular or Plural?

> The choice of singular or plural can be confusing in various situations, such as in the use of countable and uncountable nouns. This unit illustrates the main areas of difficulty and provides practice with these.

1 Five areas of difficulty

■ Find the mistake in each sentence and correct it.

(a) The proposal has both advantages and disadvantage.

(b) The majority of workers in Nigeria is under 30.

(c) There are few young people in rural area.

(d) Many places are experiencing an increase in crimes.

(e) Each companies have their own policies.

These sentences illustrate the main problem areas for international students:

(i) Nouns should agree with verbs, and pronouns with nouns:

Those problems are unique.

There are many arguments in favour.

(ii) Uncountable nouns and irregular plurals have no final 's':

Most students receive free tuition.

The main export is tropical fruit.

(iii) General statements normally use the plural:

State universities have lower fees.

(iv) 'Each/every' are followed by singular noun and verb forms:

Every **student** gets financial support.

(v) Two linked nouns should agree:

Both the **similarities** and **differences** are important.

■ Link each problem area (i–v) with one of the errors (a–e).

2 Group phrases

■ Study the following 'group' phrases.

singular + plural	plural + singular	plural + uncountable
half the universities	two types of institution	three areas of enquiry
a range of businesses	various kinds of course	several fields of research
one of the elements	many varieties of response	rates of progress

Note that if a verb has more than one subject, it must be plural, even if the preceding noun is singular:

*Scores of students, some teachers and the president **are** at the meeting.*

*Their valuable suggestions and hard work **were** vital.*

Certain 'group' nouns (e.g. team/army/government) can be followed by either a singular or plural verb:

*The team **was** defeated three times last month.* (collectively)

*The team **were** travelling by train and bus.* (separately)

3 Uncountable nouns

(a) Most nouns in English are countable, but the following are generally uncountable (i.e. they are not usually used with numbers or the plural 's').

accommodation	information	scenery
advice	knowledge	staff
behaviour	money	traffic
commerce	news	travel
data	permission	trouble

education	progress	vocabulary
equipment	research	weather
furniture	rubbish	work

NB: Many of these can be 'counted' by using an extra noun:

*Three **kinds** of commerce*

*An **item** of equipment*

*Two **members** of staff*

(b) Another group of uncountable nouns is used for materials:

wood/rubber/iron/coffee/paper/water/oil/stone

*Little **wood** is used in the construction of motor vehicles.*

*Huge amounts of **paper** are used to produce these magazines.*

Many of these nouns can be used as countable nouns with a rather different meaning:

*Over 20 daily **papers** are published in Delhi.*

*Most **woods** are home to a wide variety of birds.*

(c) The most difficult group can be used either as countable or uncountable nouns, often with quite different meanings (further examples: business/capital/experience):

*She developed an **interest** in microfinance.*

*The bank is paying 4% **interest** on six-month deposits.*

Other nouns with a similar pattern are used for general concepts (love/fear/hope):

*Most people feel that **life** is too short.* (in general)

*Nearly 20 **lives** were lost in the mining accident.* (in particular)

4 Practice A

■ **In the following sentences, choose the correct alternative.**

(a) Little/few news about the takeover was released.

(b) She established three successful businesses/business in 2009.

(c) Substantial experiences/experience of report writing are/is required for this post.

(d) It has often been claimed that travel broadens/travels broaden the mind.

(e) How much advice/many advices were they given before coming to Australia?

(f)　She had <u>little interest/few interests</u> outside her work.

(g)　The insurance policy excludes the effects of civil <u>war/wars</u>.

(h)　Electric <u>irons were/iron was</u> first produced in the twentieth century.

(i)　They studied the <u>work/works</u> of three groups of employees over two years.

5　Practice B

■　Read the text and choose the correct alternative.

E-COMMERCE

A large number of <u>company/companies</u> <u>has/have</u> developed <u>website/websites</u> in the last ten years. Trading using the internet is called <u>e-commerce/e-commerces</u>, and <u>this/these</u> <u>is/are</u> divided into two main kinds: B2B and B2C. Many <u>business/businesses</u> want to use the internet to sell directly to <u>its/their</u> customers (B2C), but large numbers have experienced <u>trouble/troubles</u> with <u>security/securities</u> and other practical issues. In addition, the high start-up costs and the <u>expense/expenses</u> of advertising <u>means/mean</u> that <u>this/these</u> <u>company/companies</u> often struggle to make a profit for some time.

Style

There is no one correct style of academic writing, but in general it should attempt to be accurate, impersonal and objective. For example, personal pronouns such as 'I' and idioms (i.e. informal language) are used less often than in other kinds of writing. Students should study examples of writing in their own subject area, and then aim to develop their own 'voice'. This unit gives guidelines for an appropriate style, and provides practice.

1 Components of academic style

■ Study this paragraph and underline any examples of poor style.

> How to make people work harder is a topic that lots of people have written about in the last few years. There are lots of different theories etc and I think some of them are ok. When we think about this we should remember the old Chinese proverb, that you can lead a horse to water but you can't make it drink. So how do we increase production? It's quite a complex subject but I'll just talk about a couple of ideas.

Some of the problems with the style of this paragraph can be analysed as follows:

Poor style	Reason
How to make people work harder . . .	Imprecise vocabulary – use 'motivation'
. . . lots of people . . .	Vague – give names
. . . the last few years.	Vague – give dates
lots of different . . .	Avoid 'lots of'
. . . etc . . .	Avoid using 'etc.' and 'so on'
. . . I think . . .	Too personal
. . . are ok.	Too informal
When we think about this . . .	Too personal
. . . the old Chinese proverb . . .	Do not quote proverbs or similar expressions
So how do we increase production?	Avoid rhetorical questions
It's quite a . . .	Avoid contractions
. . . I'll just talk about a couple . . .	Too personal and informal

The paragraph could be rewritten in a more suitable style:

> Motivation has been the subject of numerous studies during recent decades, but this essay will focus on Maslow's hierarchy of needs theory (1943) and Herzberg's two-factor theory (1966). Their contemporary relevance to the need to motivate employees effectively will be examined critically, given that this can be considered crucial to a firm's survival in the current economic climate.

2 Guidelines

There are no rules for academic style that apply to all situations. The following are guidelines that should help you develop a style of your own.

(a) Do not use idiomatic or colloquial vocabulary: *kids, boss*. Instead, use standard English: *children, manager*.

(b) Use vocabulary accurately. There is a difference between *currency* and *money*, or *governance* and *government*, which you are expected to know in your subject area.

(c) Be as precise as possible when dealing with facts or figures. Avoid phrases such as *about a hundred* or *hundreds of years ago*. If it is necessary to estimate numbers, use *approximately* rather than *about*.

(d) Conclusions should use tentative language. Avoid absolute statements such as *unemployment causes crime*. Instead, use cautious phrases: *unemployment may cause crime* or *tends to cause crime*.

(e) Avoid adverbs that show your personal attitude: *luckily, remarkably, surprisingly*.

(f) Do not contract verb forms: *don't, can't*. Use the full form: *do not, cannot*.

(g) Although academic English tends to use the passive more than standard English, it should not be overused. Both have their place. Compare:

> *Manners (1995) claims that most companies perform worse when* . . .

> *It is widely agreed that most companies perform worse when* . . .

In the first case, the focus is on the source, in the second on what companies do.

▶ **See Unit 2.9 Passives**

(h) Avoid the following:

- *like* for introducing examples – use *such as* or *for instance*.
- *thing* and combinations *nothing* or *something* – use *factor, issue* or *topic*.
- *lots of* – use *a significant/considerable number*.
- *little/big* – use *small/large*.
- 'get' phrases such as *get better/worse* – use *improve* and *deteriorate*.
- *good/bad* are simplistic – use *positive/negative* (e.g. *the changes had several positive aspects*).

(i) Do not use question forms such as *What were the reasons for the decline in wool exports?* Instead, use statements: *There were four main reasons for the decline* . . .

(j) Avoid numbering sections of your text, except in reports and long essays. Use conjunctions and signposting expressions to introduce new sections (*Turning to the question of taxation* . . .).

(k) When writing lists, avoid using *etc.* or *and so on*. Insert *and* before the last item: *The main products were pharmaceuticals, electronic goods and confectionery*.

(l) Avoid using two-word verbs such as *go on* or *bring up* if there is a suitable synonym. Use *continue* or *raise*.

▶ **See Unit 3.4 Academic Vocabulary: Verbs and Adverbs**

3 Practice A

■   In the following sentences, underline examples of bad style and rewrite them in a more suitable way.

(a)   What was the biggest thing that made Lehman Brothers collapse?

(b)   Unfortunately, I think there's a good chance of inflation increasing.

(c)   Lots of people think that the economy is getting worse.

(d)   A few years ago the price of property in Japan went down a lot.

(e)   You can't always trust the numbers in that report.

(f)   Sadly, the German inflation led to poverty, social unrest and so on.

(g)   They sacked the boss for cooking the books.

(h)   These days lots of people don't have jobs.

4 Avoiding repetition and redundancy

Instead of repeating the same word in a short text:

> *Most family businesses employ less than ten people. These businesses . . .*

Try to make the text more interesting by using synonyms:

> *Most family businesses employ less than ten people. These firms . . .*

▶   **See Unit 3.9 Synonyms**

Redundancy (i.e. repeating an idea or including an irrelevant point) suggests that the writer is not fully in control of the material. It gives the impression that either he/she does not properly understand the language or is trying to 'pad' the essay by repeating the same point. Avoid phrases such as:

> *Business schools in Spain are cheaper than business schools in the UK.*

Good writing aims for economy and precision:

> *Business schools in Spain are cheaper than in the UK.*

■ In the following text, remove all repetition and redundancy, rewriting where necessary.

FAST FOOD

Currently these days, fast food is growing in popularity. Fast food is a kind of food that people can buy or cook quickly. This essay examines the advantages of fast food and the drawbacks of fast food. First above all, fast food is usually tasty. Most of the people who work in offices are very busy, so that they do not have time to go to their homes for lunch. But the people who work in offices can eat tasty and delicious food in McDonalds' restaurants, which are franchised in hundreds of countries. In addition, the second benefit of fast food is its cheapness. As it is produced in large quantities, this high volume means that the companies can keep costs down. As a result fast food is usually less expensive than a meal in a conventional restaurant.

---

5 Varying sentence length

Short sentences are clear and easy to read:

> *Car scrappage schemes have been introduced in many countries.*

But too many short sentences are monotonous:

> *Car scrappage schemes have been introduced in many countries. They offer a subsidy to buyers of new cars. The buyers must scrap an old vehicle. The schemes are designed to stimulate the economy. They also increase fuel efficiency.*

Long sentences are more interesting but can be difficult to construct and read:

> *Car scrappage schemes, which offer a subsidy to buyers of new cars (who must scrap an old vehicle) have been introduced in many countries; the schemes are designed to stimulate the economy and also to increase fuel efficiency.*

Effective writing normally uses a mixture of long and short sentences, often using a short sentence to introduce the topic.

■ **Rewrite the following paragraph so that instead of six short sentences, there are two long and two short sentences.**

> Worldwide, enrolments in higher education are increasing. In developed countries over half of all young people enter college. Similar trends are seen in China and South America. This growth has put financial strain on state university systems. Many countries are asking students and parents to contribute. This leads to a debate about whether students or society benefit from tertiary education.

■ **The following sentence is too long. Divide it into shorter ones.**

> China is one developing country (but not the only one) which has imposed fees on students since 1997, but the results have been surprising: enrolments, especially in the most expensive universities, have continued to rise steeply, growing 200% overall between 1997 and 2011; it seems in this case that higher fees attract rather than discourage students, who see them as a sign of a good education, and compete more fiercely for places, leading to the result that a place at a good college can cost $8000 per year for fees and maintenance.

Until you feel confident in your writing, it is better to use shorter rather than longer sentences. This should make your meaning as clear as possible.

6 The use of caution

A cautious style is necessary in many areas of academic writing to avoid making statements that can be contradicted:

> Demand for healthcare **usually** exceeds supply.
>
> **Most** students find writing exam essays difficult.
>
> Fertility rates **tend** to fall as societies get richer.

Areas where caution is particularly important include:

(a) Outlining a hypothesis that needs to be tested (e.g. in an introduction).

(b) Discussing the results of a study, which may not be conclusive.

(c) Commenting on the work of other writers.

(d) Making predictions (normally with **may** or **might**).

Caution is also needed to avoid making statements that are too simplistic:

> *Workers are motivated by money.*

Such statements are rarely completely true. There is usually an exception that needs to be considered. Caution can be shown in several ways:

> *Workers **may** be motivated by money.* (modal verb)
>
> *Workers are **frequently** motivated by money.* (adverb)
>
> *Workers **tend** to be motivated by money.* (verb)

■ Complete the table below with more examples of each.

Modals	Adverbs	Verb/phrase
can	*commonly*	*tend to*

▶ See Unit 2.8 Generalisations

7 Using modifiers

Another way to express caution is to use **quite**, **rather** or **fairly** before an adjective:

> *a **fairly** accurate summary*
>
> *a **rather** inconvenient location*
>
> ***quite** a significant discovery*

NB: **quite** is often used before the article. It is generally used positively, while **rather** tends to be used negatively.

■ Insert quite/rather/fairly in the following to emphasise caution.

(a) The company's efforts to save energy were successful.

(b) The survey was a comprehensive study of student opinion.

(c) His second book had a hostile reception.

(d) The first year students were fascinated by her lectures.

(e) The latest type of mobile phone is expensive.

8 Practice B

■ Rewrite the following sentences in a more cautious way.

(a) Private companies are more efficient than state-owned businesses.

(b) Exploring space is a waste of valuable resources.

(c) Older students perform better at university than younger ones.

(d) Word-of-mouth is the best kind of advertising.

(e) English pronunciation is confusing.

(f) Most shopping will be done on the internet in ten years' time.

Visual Information

In many assignments in Business and Economics, it is essential to support your writing with statistics. Visual devices such as graphs and tables are a convenient way of displaying large quantities of numerical information in a form that is easy to understand. This unit explains and practises the language connected with these devices.

1 Types of visuals

On pp. 150–151 are examples of some of the main types of visuals used in academic texts.

■ Complete the table below to show the use (a–f) and the example (A–F) of each type.

Uses: (a) location (b) comparison (c) proportion (d) function (e) changes in time (f) statistical display

Types	Uses	Example
1 Diagram		
2 Table		
3 Map		
4 Pie chart		
5 Bar chart		
6 Line graph		

(A) Cinema ticket sales

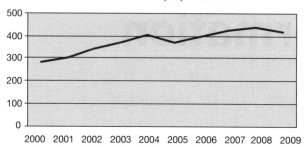

Cinema ticket sales ($m) 2000–2009

(B) Total expenditure on R&D (% of GDP)

Sweden	3.6
Finland	3.4
Iceland	3.1
Japan	3.0
South Korea	2.9
United States	2.8
Switzerland	2.6

(C) Electricity output from coal

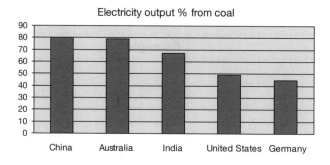

Electricity output % from coal

(D) Origins of international students

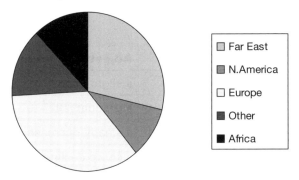

- ☐ Far East
- ☐ N.America
- ☐ Europe
- ■ Other
- ■ Africa

(E) Structure of the research unit

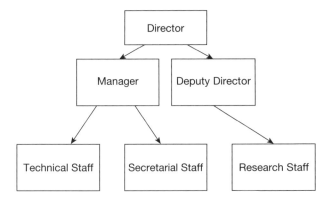

(F) Position of the main library

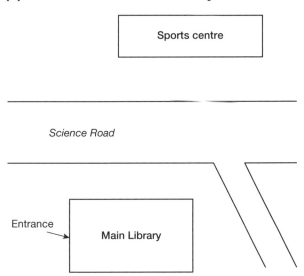

2 The language of change

(Past tenses in brackets)

Verb ⟶	Adverb	Verb ⟶	Adjective + noun
grow (grew)	slightly	drop (dropped)	a slight drop
rise (rose)	gradually	fall (fell)	a gradual fall
increase (increased)	steadily	decrease (decreased)	a steady decrease
climb (climbed)	sharply	decline (declined)	a sharp decline
also: a peak, to peak, a plateau, to level off, a trough			

> Average temperatures **rose steadily** until 2012 and then **dropped slightly**.
>
> There was a **sharp decrease** in sales during the summer and then a **gradual rise**.

■ Study the graph below and complete the following description with words from the table above.

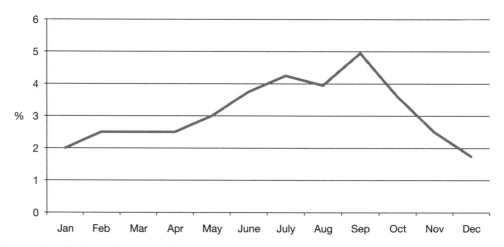

Figure 1 Inflation January–December

> The graph shows that the rate of inflation was 2% in January, and then
> (a) _____ to 2.5% in February. After that it (b) _____ until April,
> and then (c) _____ (d) _____ to over 4% in July. Inflation fell
> (e) _____ in August, but (f) _____ to a (g) _____ of 5%
> in September. Subsequently, it (h) _____ (i) _____ to below 2%
> in December.

3 Describing visuals

Although visuals do largely speak for themselves, it is common to help the reader interpret them by briefly commenting on their main features.

The	graph	shows	the changes in the price of oil since 1990.
	map	illustrates	the main sources of copper in Africa.
	diagram	displays	the organisation of both companies.

■ **(a) Read the following descriptions of the chart below. Which is better?**

(i)   The chart shows the quantity of tea consumed by the world's leading tea consuming nations. India and China together consume more than half the world's tea production, with India alone consuming about one third. Other significant tea consumers are Turkey, Russia and Britain. 'Others' includes the United States, Iran and Egypt.

(ii) The chart shows that 31% of the world's tea is consumed by India, 23% by China, and 8% by Turkey. The fourth largest consumers are Russia, Japan and Britain, with 7% each, while Pakistan consumes 5%. Other countries account for the remaining 12%.

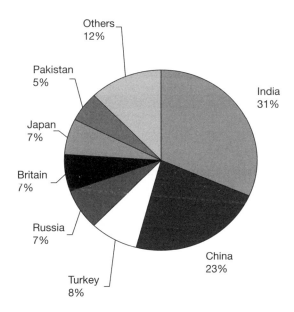

Figure 2 World tea consumption

Source: The Tea Council

■   **(b) Complete the description of the chart below.**

The bar chart shows population (a) _____ in a variety of countries around the world. It (b) _____ the extreme contrast (c) _____ crowded nations such as South Korea (475 people per sq. km.) and much (d) _____ countries such as Canada (3 people per sq. km.). Clearly, climate plays a major (e) _____ in determining population density, (f) _____ the least crowded nations (g) _____ to have extreme climates (e.g. cold in Russia or dry in Algeria).

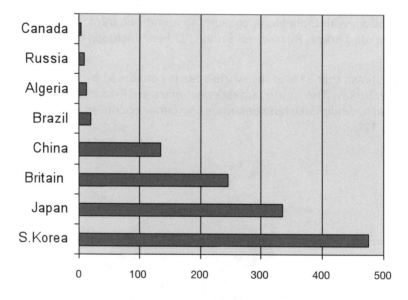

Figure 3 Population density (people per square kilometre)
Source: OECD

4 Labelling

*   When referring to visual information in the text, the word 'figure' is used for almost everything (such as maps, charts and graphs) except tables.
*   Figures and tables should be numbered and given a title. Titles of tables are written above, while titles of figures are written below the data.
*   As with other data, sources must be given for all visual information.
*   If you are writing a lengthy work such as a dissertation, you will need to provide lists of tables and figures, showing numbers, titles and page numbers, after the contents page.

5 Practice A

■ Complete the following description of the table below (one word per gap).

Table 1 Government taxation 2010

	Australia	Brazil	China	France	Germany	India	Japan	Russia	UK	USA
Total tax as % GDP	29.5	32.3	16.4	44.7	40.4	18.9	28.2	33.2	37.7	28.0

Source: OECD

Table 1 (a) _____ the proportion of tax revenues raised by national governments in relation to GDP in 2010. It can be seen that there are considerable variations, with the (b) _____ government collecting nearly 45% of GDP, while in China the (c) _____ is below 20%. In general, (d) _____ with higher welfare spending such as France, Germany and the UK collect more (e) _____ the developing BRIC economies such as India, but there are some exceptions to this, with the Brazilian government collecting a (f) _____ percentage of GDP than Australia's.

6 Practice B

■ Write a paragraph commenting on the data in the table below.

Table 2 The world's largest companies by revenue, 2013

Rank	Company	Industry	Revenues $bn.
1	Wal-Mart Stores	Retail	476
2	Royal Dutch Shell	Oil	451
3	China National Petroleum	Oil	425
4	Exxon Mobile	Oil	420
5	Synopec	Oil	411
6	BP	Oil	379
7	Saudi Aramco	Oil	311
8	Vitol	Commodities	303
9	State Grid Corp of China	Electricity supply	290
10	Total	Oil	240

Source: *Fortune* magazine

Revision Exercise
Elements of Writing

■ Answer the following questions, which revise some of the material in Part 2.

1   Give three synonyms for 'disadvantage'.

2   Rewrite in an impersonal way:

I think that the traditional high street shop is becoming redundant.

3   Underline the counterargument in this sentence:

State-owned companies are often seen as inefficient, but certain industries do involve a 'natural monopoly'.

4   Write two sentences showing a link between these situations:

• an increase in house prices

• rising demand for housing

5   In the following, link the reference words to the words they refer to:

The Rolls-Royce Company was founded in 1906. It was the creation of two men, Henry Royce and Charles Rolls. The former was an engineer, the latter a salesman. When demand for their cars grew, they built a new factory at Derby, which was opened in 1908.

6   Write three sentences comparing a Rolls Royce car with a Toyota Prius.

7   List eight situations where the definite article is always used (e.g. 'the dollar' – currencies).

8   Write simple definitions for:

(a) a graduate

(b) a scholarship

(c) a limited company

9   Rewrite the following with suitable phrases to introduce the examples in brackets.

(a) A few districts are famous for technological innovation. (Silicon Valley)

(b) Certain inventions have changed the way we live. (mobile phones)

(c) Some successful entrepreneurs have had little formal business education. (Richard Branson)

10   What are the two ways of making a generalisation? Give examples.

11   Write two sentences, one active and one passive, using the information below.

Google	1996	began	as research project	by Page and Brin

12   Punctuate the following:

the twentyfirst century has seen the rise of the bric economies brazil russia india and china the acronym was first used in a paper written by jim oneill in 2001

13   What are the three main aims of good academic style?

14   What are the following visuals usually used to show?

(a) line graph

(b) diagram

(c) pie chart

(d) table

Vocabulary for Writing

Approaches to Vocabulary

1 Introduction

International students of Business may be understandably concerned by the quantity and complexity of the vocabulary required for reading academic texts. But it is worth remembering that much of that vocabulary is specific to your subject area, and probably already quite familiar to you. For example, in the sentence:

*The **effectiveness** of **management buy-outs** has been a subject of **controversy**.*

'Management buy-outs' is a term specific to Business, while 'effectiveness' and 'controversy' are general academic vocabulary that all students need to understand.

But developing vocabulary involves more than learning lists of words. Part 3, Vocabulary for Writing, provides a variety of approaches to improving students' understanding in this area.

■ This paragraph illustrates some of the vocabulary difficulties facing students when reading and writing academic texts. Read it carefully, paying particular attention to words in bold.

GOING TO EXTREMES?

Muller (2012) **maintains** that the increased frequency of extreme weather events is linked to global warming, **in particular** to rising sea temperatures. **However**, McKenzie (2013) **insists** Muller has **a bee in his bonnet** on this topic, caused by using a **dysfunctional** model, and that there is no real evidence that **phenomena** such as flooding and hurricanes are becoming more common. He considers that the **key** issue is the growing population in areas vulnerable to events such as floods. Muller's **principal** concern is a rise in the temperature of the north Pacific Ocean of

0.5° **C** since 1968, which McKenzie regards as being within the normal range of historical fluctuation. But Javez (2009) and Simmonds (2011), *inter alia*, have argued for an international research programme under the auspices of **UNESCO** to monitor these events, given the **threefold** rise in the cost of insurance claims since 2000.

■ Study the table below, which shows where each vocabulary issue is dealt with more fully.

Line	Item	Vocabulary issue	Unit
1 3	maintains insists	referring verbs for summarising ideas	3.4 Academic Vocabulary: Verbs and Adverbs
2	in particular however	conjunctions	3.5 Conjunctions
3	a bee in his bonnet	idiom	3.1 Approaches to Vocabulary
4	dysfunctional	can be understood by the prefix	3.7 Prefixes and Suffixes
4	phenomena	approximate synonym for 'events'	3.9 Synonyms
5	key	metaphor	3.1 Approaches to Vocabulary
7	principal	often confused with 'principle'	3.1 Approaches to Vocabulary
7 11	0.5° C threefold	numerical information	3.6 Numbers
9	*inter alia*	phrase from another language	3.1 Approaches to Vocabulary
10	UNESCO	abbreviation	3.2 Abbreviations

2 Language features

The following words (all nouns) are used to describe common features of language.

■ **Discuss the words in the list with a partner. Try to think of an example of each.**

Ambiguity	*Where more than one meaning is possible; lack of clarity*
Anecdote	*A story told to illustrate a situation or idea*
Cliché	*An overused idea or phrase; lacking in freshness*
Euphemism	*Word or phrase used to avoid the naming of something embarrassing directly*
Exaggeration	*Making something better or worse than the reality*
Idiom	*Common phrase used in colloquial speech, meaning of which is not obvious*
Metaphor	*A word used to describe something different from the original meaning*
Paradox	*An idea that seems wrong but yet may be true*
Proverb	*A traditional statement or rhyme containing advice or a moral*
Saying	*An often-repeated comment that seems to contain some truth*
Simile	*A comparison of two things, using 'like' or 'as'*
Slogan	*A frequently repeated phrase used in advertising or politics*
Statement	*A rather formal comment on a situation*
Synopsis	*A summary of something*
Understatement	*Saying less than you feel; the opposite of exaggeration*

3 Practice

■ Study the following sentences and decide which of the features listed on p. 163 each illustrates.

(a) He said that getting a B minus for his essay had been the worst shock of his life. (__exaggeration__)

(b) The President said she regretted the loss of life in the disaster and sympathised with the survivors. (_____)

(c) At the beginning of the lecture, Professor Chang told them about the strange habits of her first boss. (_____)

(d) He warned them that there was no such thing as a free lunch. (_____)

(e) The author of the report passed away on 21 November. (_____)

(f) He told the class that their Economics course was a voyage over an uncharted ocean. (_____)

(g) After his laptop was stolen, with the only copy of his dissertation on it, he said he felt rather annoyed. (_____)

(h) She said that the older she got, the less she seemed to know. (_____)

(i) After the price rise, sales fell like a stone. (_____)

(j) It is said that the early bird catches the worm. (_____)

(k) Their teacher explained that the project consisted of two parts; the first a literature review, the second a survey report. (_____)

(l) He was over the moon when he won the scholarship. (__idiom__)

(m) 'Finger lickin' good' has sold millions of chicken meals. (_____)

(n) His feelings towards his old school were a mixture of love and hate. (_____)

(o) Paris is the capital of romance; the city for lovers. (_____)

4 Confusing pairs

Certain common words cause confusion because they have similar but distinct spellings and meanings:

> *The drought **affected** the wheat harvest in Australia.*

> *An immediate **effect** of the price rise was a fall in demand.*

'Affect' and 'effect' are two different words. 'Affect' is a verb, while 'effect' is commonly used as a noun.

■ Study the differences between other similar confusing pairs (most common use in brackets).

accept (verb/except (prep)
It is difficult to accept their findings.
The report is finished except for the conclusion.

compliment (noun/verb)/complement (verb)
Her colleagues complimented her on her presentation.
His latest book complements his previous research on African consumers.

economic (adj)/economical (adj)
Inflation was one economic result of the war.
Sharing a car to go to work was an economical move.

its (pronoun)/it's (pronoun + verb)
It's widely agreed that carbon emissions are rising.
The car's advanced design was its most distinct feature.

lose (verb)/loose (adj)
No general ever plans to lose a battle.
He stressed the loose connection between HRM and Psychology.

principal (adj/noun)/principle (noun)
All economists recognise the principle of supply and demand.
Zurich is the principal city of Switzerland.

rise (verb – past tense rose)/raise (verb – past tense raised)
The population of Sydney rose by 35% in the century.
The university raised its fees by 10% last year.

site (noun)/sight (noun)
The site of the battle is now covered by an airport.
The new office block was an impressive sight.

tend to (verb)/trend (noun)
Students tend to enjoy watching movies.
In many countries, there is a trend towards smaller families.

■ Choose the correct word in each sentence.

(a) The company was founded on the principals/principles of quality and value.

(b) Millions of people are attempting to lose/loose weight.

(c) Sunspots have been known to affect/effect radio communication.

(d) Professor Poledna received their compliments/complements politely.

(e) Both social and economical/economic criteria need to be examined.

(f) It took many years for some of Keynes' theories to be accepted/excepted.

5 Words and phrases from other languages

When reading academic texts, you may meet words and phrases from other languages, usually Latin, German or French. They are generally used because there is no exact English equivalent, and they are often printed in italics:

> While the basic tripartite division of the theory into *jus ad bellum, jus in bello* and *jus post-bellum,* and the criteria related to each . . .

(meaning: reasons for going to war, laws of warfare and rules for post-war)

You are not expected to use these phrases in your own writing, but it is useful to understand them when you read. They can be found in a dictionary, but some of the more common are listed below:

Latin

ad hoc	unplanned
de facto	as it really is
de jure	according to law
inter alia	among others
pro rata	proportional

French

à propos	on the subject of
ancien regime	old ruling system
coup d'état	military takeover
fait accompli	accomplished fact
raison d'être	reason for living

German

Mittelstand	small and medium-sized companies
Mitteleuropa	central Europe
Realpolitik	political reality
Zeitgeist	spirit of the times

Abbreviations

Abbreviations are an important and expanding feature of contemporary English, widely used for convenience and space saving. Students need to be familiar with general, academic and business abbreviations.

1 Types of abbreviations

Abbreviations take the form of shortened words, acronyms or other abbreviations, as shown below.

(a) **Shortened words** are often used without the writer being aware of the original form. 'Ad' and 'advert' come from 'advertisement', which is rarely used in modern English. However, 'refrigerator' is still better in written English than the informal 'fridge'. 'Public house' is now very formal ('pub' is acceptable), but 'television' or 'TV' should be used instead of the idiomatic 'telly'.

(b) **Acronyms** are made up of the initial letters of a name or phrase (e.g. SWOT = Strengths, Weaknesses, Opportunities, Threats). They are pronounced as words.

(c) **Other abbreviations** are read as sets of individual letters. They include names of countries, organisations and companies (USA/BBC), and also abbreviations that are only found in written English (e.g. PTO means please turn over). Note that in many cases, abbreviations are widely used without most users knowing what the individual letters stand for (e.g. DNA, DVD).

2 Business abbreviations

As with all academic subjects, Business and Economics employ abbreviations to save time and space. Common examples include:

AGM	annual general meeting
B2B	business to business
CEO	chief executive officer
CV	curriculum vitae
DIY	do-it-yourself (retail sector)
EPS	earnings per share
GNP	gross national product
HRM	human resource management
ICT	information and communications technology
IMF	International Monetary Fund
IPO	initial public offering
IOU	I owe you
M&A	mergers and acquisitions
PLC	public limited company
PPP	purchasing power parity
PR	public relations
R&D	research and development
SOE	state-owned enterprise
SME	small or medium enterprise
RPI	retail prices index
TQM	total quality management
USP	unique selling point
VC	venture capital
WTO	World Trade Organisation

Depending on the area of study, it is also useful to be familiar with abbreviations for major companies and organisations, for example (in the UK):

BT	British Telecom
FCA	Financial Conduct Authority
NHS	National Health Service
RBS	Royal Bank of Scotland
UCL	University College London

However, writers will also employ more specialised abbreviations in texts, which should be explained in brackets on first use:

Starting from the resource-based view (RBV) of the firm, it is argued that . . .

The Technology Readiness Index (TRI) was introduced by Parasuraman (2000).

3 Punctuation

There are many standard abbreviations that have a full stop after them to show that it is a shortened form (lt. = litre). Other examples are govt. (government), co. (company) and Oct. (October). With acronyms and other abbreviations, it is now normal to write the letters without full stops (e.g. LSE, UN).

4 Duplicate abbreviations

Abbreviations can be confusing. DJ normally stands for 'disc jockey', but in business refers to the Dow Jones Index. GM means General Motors but also 'genetically modified'. LSE may mean the London Stock Exchange or the London School of Economics. It is useful to be aware of these potential confusions. A good dictionary should be used to understand more unusual abbreviations.

5 Abbreviations in writing

Certain abbreviations are found in all types of academic writing. They include:

anon.	anonymous (author unknown)
asap	as soon as possible
c.	circa (in dates – about)
cf.	compare
ed.	editor/edition
e.g.	for example
et al.	and others (used for giving names of multiple authors)
etc.	etcetera (and so on – do not use this in academic work)
Fig.	figure (for labelling charts and graphs)
ibid.	in the same place (to refer to source mentioned immediately before)
i.e.	that is
K	thousand
NB	take careful note
nd.	no date (i.e. an undated source)
op. cit.	in the source mentioned previously
p.a.	yearly (per annum)
pp.	pages
P.S.	postscript
re.	with reference to
vs.	versus

6 Practice

■ Explain the abbreviations in the following sentences.

(a) The failure rate among ICT projects in SOEs reaches 70% (Smith *et al.*, 2008).

(b) The new laptop's USP was its radical design.

(c) The world's most populous country (i.e. China) joined the WTO in 2001.

(d) NB: CVs must be submitted to HR by 30 June.

(e) See the OECD's recent report on the UAE.

(f)   The EU hopes to achieve a standard rate of VAT.

(g) The CEO intends to raise spending on R&D by 40%.

(h) Fig. 4. Trade patterns on the www (2009–2014).

(i)   BA has opened a new route to HK via KL.

(j)   Director of PR required – salary approx. $75K.

(k) Re. the AGM next month: the report is needed asap.

(l)   Prof. Wren claimed that the quality of MSc and PhD research was falling.

Academic Vocabulary

Nouns and Adjectives

To read and write academic papers effectively, students need to be familiar with the rather formal vocabulary widely used in this area. This unit focuses on nouns and adjectives; Unit 3.4 looks at verbs and adverbs.

1 Nouns

■ Study the following list of common academic nouns, with examples of use. With a partner, find an approximate synonym for each noun.

accuracy	*Repeating the experiment will improve the **accuracy** of the process.*
analysis	*His **analysis of** the results showed a high level of employee dissatisfaction.*
approach	*Professor Han has brought a new **approach** to the study of accounting.*
assessment	*She failed the first module **assessment** but passed the final one.*
assumption	*He made the **assumption** that all the students spoke French.*
authority	*Dr James is our leading **authority** on labour law.*

category	Her work established two **categories** of corporate governance.
claim	Their **claim** that the company was founded in the 1700s is false.
controversy	Climate change is an issue that has caused much **controversy**.
correlation	They found a **correlation** between height and wealth.
deterrent	Weak consumer demand acted as a **deterrent** to expansion.
emphasis	Their teacher put the **emphasis** on practical research.
evidence	The fall in profits provided **evidence** of his poor management.
exception	The Tesla is an **exception** to the idea of slow, small electric cars.
extract	He read a short **extract** from his paper on Friedman to the class.
ideology	Military power was at the heart of Roman **ideology**.
implication	The **implication** of the report is that we need to do more research.
innovation	Steam power was a significant **innovation** in the eighteenth century.
intuition	**Intuition** has been described as 'a gut feeling'.
motivation	Money is often claimed to be the **motivation** for most workers.
perspective	Sigmund Freud's work opened a new **perspective** on human behaviour.
phenomenon	Earthquakes are an unusual **phenomenon** in Britain.
policy	The university has a zero-tolerance **policy** on plagiarism.
preference	Her **preference** was criminal law, but other fields were more profitable.
process	The product evaluation **process** took two years.
proposal	The professor's **proposal** for more seminars was rejected.
provision	The library has increased its **provision** of computer terminals by 100%.
sequence	Writing is a **sequence** of reading, note-taking, planning and drafting.
strategy	Swimming every day was part of his **strategy** for getting fit.
substitute	To what extent can natural gas be a **substitute** for oil?
technique	She developed a new **technique** for measuring innovation.
validity	Events confirmed the **validity** of his prediction.

■ **Complete each sentence with a suitable noun.**

(a) The enquiry found no _____ of corruption in the tendering process.

(b) The tutor asked the class for their _____ for next semester's topics.

(c) Many great discoveries were based on _____ rather than logic.

(d) Due to the rising birth rate, _____ was made for more school places.

(e) The study suggested a weak _____ between juice sales and hot weather.

2 Using nouns and adjectives

It is easy to confuse the noun and adjective form of words such as 'possible' and 'possibility'.

■ **Compare these sentences:**

> The **efficiency** of the machine depends on the **precision** of its construction.
>
> **Precise** construction results in an **efficient** machine.

The first sentence uses the nouns 'efficiency' and 'precision'. The second uses adjectives: 'precise' and 'efficient'. Although the meaning is similar, the first sentence is more formal. Effective academic writing requires accurate use of both nouns and adjectives.

■ **Complete the gaps in the table below.**

Noun	Adjective	Noun	Adjective
approximation	approximate		particular
superiority		reason	
	strategic		synthetic
politics		economics/economy*	
	industrial		cultural
exterior		average	
	high		reliable
heat		strength	
	confident		true
width		probability	
	necessary		long
danger		relevance	

* Compare the three nouns:

> **Economics** *is a demanding undergraduate degree course.* (academic subject)
> *The Greek* **economy** *is heavily in debt.* (national economy, countable)
> **Economy** *is needed to reduce the deficit.* (saving money, uncountable)

3 Practice A

■ Insert a suitable noun or adjective from the table on p. 174 into each sentence.

(a) The students were _____ their project would be successful.

(b) One of Tokyo's _____ is its excellent transport system.

(c) There is a strong _____ that fees will rise next year.

(d) The students complained that the lecture was not _____ to their course.

(e) The results are so surprising it will be _____ to repeat the experiment.

(f) The _____ household size in Turkey is 4.1.

(g) Regularly backing up computer files reduces the _____ of losing vital work.

(h) Revising for exams is a tedious _____.

(i) These data appear to be _____ and should not be trusted.

(j) The _____ sales figure for the year will be about three million.

(k) The _____ consequences of the war were inflation and unemployment.

(l) They attempted to make a _____ of all the different proposals.

4 Academic adjectives

The following adjectives are best understood and learnt as opposites:

absolute	*relative*
abstract	*concrete*
accurate	*inaccurate*
ambiguous	*unambiguous*
analytic	*synthetic*
effective	*ineffective*
exclusive	*inclusive*
logical	*illogical*
metaphorical	*literal*
precise	*vague* or *approximate* or *rough*

rational	*irrational*
reliable	*unreliable*
relevant	*irrelevant*
specific	*non-specific*
subjective	*objective*
theoretical	*practical* or *empirical* or *pragmatic*

*Inflation is an **abstract** concept.*

*The **metaphorical** use of the word 'key' is probably more common than its **literal** one.*

*The study of mathematics is highly **relevant** to economics.*

*Her study of women in management roles was criticised for being too **subjective**.*

*In Europe, **empirical** research began in the sixteenth century.*

5 Practice B

■ Complete each sentence with a suitable adjective from the table in section 4.

(a) The teacher complained that the quotes were _____ to the title.

(b) His _____ approach led him to ignore some inconvenient facts.

(c) _____examples are needed to make the argument clear.

(d) It is sufficient to give _____ figures for national populations.

(e) Poverty is usually regarded as a _____ concept.

(f) They approached the task in a _____ way by first analysing the title.

(g) The students preferred examining case studies to _____ discussion.

(h) The results were _____: the new product range was a failure.

6 Practice C

■ Underline the adjective in each sentence and write the related noun in brackets.

Example: Several steel producers are <u>likely</u> to shut down next year. (__*likelihood*__)

(a) The HR team have just completed a strategic review of pay. (_____)

(b) Dr Lee adopted an analytical approach to the inquiry. (_____)

(c) Nylon was one of the earliest synthetic fibres. (_____)

(d) Her major contribution to the research was her study of coal mining.
     (_____)

(e) All advertising must respect cultural differences. (_____)

(f) Some progress was made in the theoretical area. (_____)

(g) A frequent complaint is that too much reading is expected. (_____)

(h) We took a more critical approach to marketing theory. (_____)

(i) The Department of Social Policy is offering three courses this year.
      (_____)

(j) Finally, the practical implications of my findings will be examined.
      (_____)

Students wishing to develop their academic vocabulary should study the Academic Word List (AWL). This is a list of 570 items commonly found in academic texts across various disciplines, created by Averil Coxhead.

See Sandra Haywood's website for information about the AWL, with further practice exercises: www.nottingham.ac.uk/~alzsh3/acvocab/.

Academic Vocabulary

Verbs and Adverbs

When reading a text, it is useful to identify and understand the main verb: this is often the key to understanding the whole sentence. This unit looks at the more formal verbs used in academic writing, the verbs of reference used to introduce summaries, and outlines the use of adverbs.

1 Understanding main verbs

■ Study the following sentence and underline the two main verbs.

> *The government has consistently encouraged entrepreneurship through courses in schools and colleges, and has considerably reduced the barriers to starting a business by eliminating bureaucratic requirements.*

To follow the writer's meaning, the reader needs to be clear that 'encouraged' and 'reduced' are the main verbs in the two parts of the sentence.
Academic writing tends to use rather formal verbs to express the writer's meaning accurately:

> *In the last decade the pace of change has **accelerated**.*

> *Could Darwin have **envisaged** the controversy his work has caused?*

In spoken English, we are more likely to use 'speed up' and 'imagined'.

■   **Study the list below and find a synonym in each case.**

NB: Some of these verbs (e.g. 'hold') are used in academic writing with a special meaning.

Verb	Example of use	Synonym
to adapt	the tax system has been **adapted** from Norway	*modified*
to arise	a similar situation **arises** when we look at new companies	
to conduct	the largest study was **conducted** in Canada	
to characterise	developing countries are **characterised** by . . .	
to clarify	the project was designed to **clarify** these contradictions	
to concentrate on	that study **concentrated on** female managers	
to be concerned with	the programme is **concerned** primarily **with** . . .	
to demonstrate	further research has **demonstrated** that few factors . . .	
to determine	the water content was experimentally **determined**	
to discriminate	a failure to **discriminate** between the two systems	
to establish	the business was **established** in 1955	
to exhibit	half of the businesses **exhibited** signs of improvement	
to focus on	her work **focused on** short-term loans	
to generate	a question which has **generated** a range of responses	
to hold	Newton's second law, $F = ma$, **holds** everywhere	
to identify	three main areas have been **identified**	
to imply	his absence **implies** a lack of interest	
to interact	understand how the two systems **interact**	
to interpret	the result can be **interpreted** as a limited success	

to manifest	as **manifested** in increased business failures	
to overcome	both difficulties were **overcome** in the first week	
to propose	they **propose** offering two new courses next year	
to prove	the use of solar power is **proving** successful	
to recognise	he is now **recognised** as a leading expert	
to relate to	the pattern was **related to** both social and physical factors	
to supplement	the research was **supplemented** by several surveys	
to undergo	the system **underwent** major changes in the 1980s	
to yield	both surveys **yielded** mixed results	

2 Using verbs of reference

Referring verbs are used to summarise another writer's ideas:

> *Previn **argued** that interest rates were too low.*

> *Bakewell (1992) **found** that most managers tended to use traditional terms . . .*

They may also be used to introduce a quotation:

> *As Scott **observed**: 'Comment is free but facts are sacred.'*

Most of these verbs are followed by a noun clause beginning with 'that'.

(a) The following mean that the writer is presenting a case:

- argue
- claim
- consider
- hypothesise
- suggest
- believe
- think
- state.

> *Melville (2007) **suggested** that tax rates should be harmonised.*

(b) A second group describe a reaction to a previously stated position:

- accept
- admit
- agree with
- deny
- doubt.

*Handlesmith **doubts** Melville's suggestion that tax rates should be harmonised.*

(c) Others include:

- assume
- conclude
- discover
- explain
- imply
- indicate
- maintain
- presume
- reveal
- show.

*Patel (2003) **assumes** that inflation will remain low.*

3 Practice A

■ Write a sentence referring to what the following writers said. (More than one verb may be suitable. Use the past tense.)

Example: Z: 'My research shows that biofuels are environmentally neutral'.
               Z **claimed/argued** that biofuels were environmentally neutral.

(a) A: 'I may have made a mistake in my calculations of the cost of living'.

(b) B: 'I did not say that women make better economists than men'.

(c) C: 'Small firms are more dynamic than large ones'.

(d) D: 'I support C's views on small firms'.

(e) E: 'I'm not sure, but most people probably work to earn money'.

(f) F: 'After much research, I've found that growing wheat is more profitable than growing potatoes'.

(g) G: 'I think it unlikely that electric cars will replace conventional ones'.

(h) H: 'There may be a link between age and entrepreneurial ability'.

4 Further referring verbs

A small group of verbs is followed by the pattern (**somebody/thing + for + noun/gerund**):

- blame
- censure
- commend
- condemn
- criticise.

> *Lee (1998)* **blamed** *the media for creating uncertainty.*

NB: All except 'commend' have a negative meaning.

Another group is followed by (**somebody/thing + as + noun/gerund**):

- assess
- characterise
- classify
- define
- describe
- evaluate
- identify
- interpret
- portray
- present.

> *Terry* **interprets** *rising oil prices as a result of the Asian recovery.*

5 Practice B

■ Rewrite the following statements using verbs from the lists in section 4.

Example: K: 'Guttman's work is responsible for many of the current social problems'.
   K **blamed** Guttman's work for many of the current social problems.

(a) L: 'She was very careless about her research methods'.

(b) M: 'There are four main types of government bonds'.

(c) N: 'That company has an excellent record for workplace safety'.

(d) O: 'Falling unemployment must be a sign of economic recovery'.

(e) P: 'Wind power and biomass will be the leading green energy sources'.

(f) Q: 'Adam Smith was the most influential economist of the eighteenth century'.

6 Using adverbs

In the sentence given in section 1, adverbs are used to give information about time (consistently) and degree (considerably):

> *The government has **consistently** encouraged entrepreneurship through courses in schools and colleges, and has **considerably** reduced the barriers to starting a business by eliminating bureaucratic requirements.*

1 Adverbs are used in academic writing in a variety of ways. Among the most important are:

(a) to provide more detail, with verbs and adjectives:

> ***Reasonably** good data are available for only . . .*

> *Economists **traditionally** argued for import controls.*

(b) individually, often at the beginning of sentences, to introduce new points or link sentences together:

> ***Currently**, the Earth's atmosphere appears to be warming up.*

> ***Alternatively**, the use of non-conventional renewable energies . . .*

NB: Adverbs used individually need to be employed with care. It is dangerous to overuse them, since they are often like the author's 'voice', commenting on the topic. As the academic writer aims to be objective, adverbs such as 'fortunately' or 'remarkably' may be unsuitable.

2 Adverbs linked to verbs and adjectives usually fall into three groups:

(a) time (when?)

> ***previously** published*

> ***retrospectively** examined*

(b) degree (how much?)

> *declined **considerably***

> *contribute **substantially***

(c) manner (in what way?)

> ***financially** complicated*

> ***remotely** located*

Further common examples include:

Time	Degree	Manner
recently	clearly	(un)surprisingly
increasingly	particularly	factually
originally	broadly	politically
presently	highly	locally
currently	wholly	alternatively
traditionally	crucially	similarly
continuously	emphatically	psychologically

7 Practice C

■ **Insert a suitable adverb from the table above into the gaps in the sentences.**

(a) The new, low-cost mobile phone was popular, _____ with the young.

(b) _____, the internet was mainly used for academic purposes.

(c) Some courses are assessed purely by exams. _____, coursework may be employed.

(d) _____, there has been growing concern about financing the health service.

(e) There was strong opposition _____ to the proposal to build the dam.

(f) _____, the development should be acceptable environmentally.

Conjunctions

Conjunctions are words or phrases that join parts of a sentence together, or link a sentence to the next one. Effective reading and writing requires clarity about their meaning. This unit describes the different functions of conjunctions and practises their use. Other ways of linking sections of text are explained in Unit 2.3 Cohesion.

1 Types of conjunctions

Note the way conjunctions work in the following sentences:

Demand for food is increasing **because** *the population is growing.*

Mechanisation has increased crop yields, **yet** *production is still inadequate.*

In the first sentence, 'because' introduces a reason, in the second 'yet' indicates opposition.

■ Underline the conjunctions in the following sentences.

(a) A few inventions, for instance television, have had a major impact on everyday life.

(b) In addition, a large volume of used cars are sold through dealerships.

(c) The definition of motivation is important since it is the cause of some disagreement.

(d) The technology allows consumers a choice, thus increasing their sense of satisfaction.

(e) Four hundred people were interviewed for the survey, then the results were analysed.

(f) However, another body of opinion associates globalisation with unfavourable outcomes.

■ There are six main types of conjunction. Match each of the types below to one of the sentences opposite.

(i)   Addition   (_6_)

(ii) Result   (___)

(iii) Reason   (___)

(iv) Opposition   (___)

(v)   Example   (___)

(vi) Time   (___)

▶ See Units 2.2 Cause and Effect and 2.7 Examples

2 Practice A

When reading a text, conjunctions are like signposts to help the reader follow the ideas.

■ Read the paragraph below and underline the conjunctions, then decide what their functions are (i.e. types i–vi above). Complete the table on p. 186.

BIOFUELS

Newly published research examines some important questions about the growing use of biofuels, <u>such as</u> ethanol made from maize. The production of these has increased sharply recently, but the replacement of food crops with these fuel crops has been heavily criticised. Although initially seen as a more environmentally-friendly type of fuel, the research shows that producing some biofuels, for instance biodiesel palm oil, is more polluting than using conventional oil. The ethanol produced from sugar cane, however, can have negative emissions, in other words taking carbon dioxide from the atmosphere instead of adding it. Consequently, it can be seen that the situation is rather confused, and that biofuels are neither a magic solution to the energy problem, nor are they the environmental disaster sometimes suggested.

Conjunction	Type	Conjunction	Type
(a) such as	example	(f)	
(b)		(g)	
(c)		(h)	
(d)		(i)	
(e)		(j)	

3 Common conjunctions

■   Working with a partner, complete the table with as many examples of conjunctions as possible.

Addition	Result	Reason	Opposition	Example	Time
moreover also					

4 Practice B

■   Insert a suitable conjunction into each gap.

(a) _____ checking the equipment, the experiment was repeated.

(b) _____ most people use the train, a minority walk or cycle.

(c) Brick is a thermally efficient building material. It is, _____, cheap.

(d) Demand has increased for summer courses, _____ extra ones are offered this year.

(e) Many writers, _____ Chekhov, have been doctors.

(f) _____ the increase in residence fees, more students are moving out.

(g) _____ the student was in the lecture, her car was being repaired.

(h) _____ he was studying Italian, he spent a semester in Bologna.

5 Conjunctions of opposition

In some ways, these are the most important type of conjunction, and can be the most difficult to use accurately. Note the position of the conjunctions in the following examples:

*The economy is strong, **but/yet** there are frequent strikes.*

***Although/while** there are frequent strikes, the economy is strong.*

***In spite of/despite** the frequent strikes, the economy is strong.*

*There are frequent strikes. **However/nevertheless,** the economy is strong.*

■ Write two sentences in each case.

Example: The equipment was expensive/unreliable.
            *The equipment was expensive **but** unreliable.*
            ***Although** the equipment was expensive, it was unreliable.*

(a) The government claimed that inflation was falling. The opposition said it was rising.

(i) _____

(ii) _____

(b) This department must reduce expenditure. It needs to install new computers.

(i) _____

(ii) _____

(c) Sales of the new car were poor. It was heavily advertised.

(i) _____

(ii) _____

6 Practice C

■ Finish the sentences in a suitable way.

(a) In contrast to America, where car ownership is widespread,

(b) Despite leaving school at the age of 14,

(c) The majority displayed a positive attitude to the proposal, but

(d) While the tutor insisted that the essay was easy,

(e) Although the spring was cold and dry,

(f) Nobody expected the restaurant to succeed, yet

Numbers

Business and Economics students need to be able to write about statistical data clearly and accurately. This unit explains and practises the basic language of numbers and percentages, while presenting data in charts and tables is dealt with in Unit 2.14 Visual Information.

1 The language of numbers

In introductions, numbers are often used to give an accurate account of a situation:

> *Women account for fewer than 2% of Fortune 500 CEOs, 14% of Fortune 500 directors, and 8% and 5% of board directors and top managers, respectively, of the biggest west European companies.*

Figures and **numbers** are both used to talk about statistical data in a general sense:

> *The figures/numbers in the report need to be read critically.*

But number is used more widely:

> *She forgot her mobile phone number.*

Digits are individual numbers:

> 4,539 – a four-**digit** number

Both **fractions** (½) and **decimals** (0.975) may be used.

There is no final 's' on hundred/thousand/million used with whole numbers:

> *Six million people live there.*

But:

> **Thousands of** *companies were formed in the dotcom boom.*

When writing about **currencies**, write *$440 m.* (440 million dollars).

Rates are normally expressed as percentages (e.g. *the rate of inflation fell to 2.5%*) but may also be per thousand (e.g. *the Austrian birth rate is 8.7*).

It is normal to write whole numbers as words from one to ten and as digits above ten:

> *Five people normally work in the café, but at peak times this can rise to 14.*

2 Percentages

These are commonly used for expressing degrees of change:

> *Between 2008 and 2012, the number of female managers rose by 10%.*

■ **Complete the following sentences using the data in the table below.**

(a   Between 2010 and 2011, the number of overseas students increased by
   _____ %.

(b) The number increased by _____ % the following year.

(c) Between 2010 and 2013, there was a _____ % increase.

Overseas students in the university 2010–2013

2010	2011	2012	2013
200	300	600	1,000

3 Simplification

Although the accurate use of numbers is vital, too many statistics can make texts difficult to read. If the actual number is not important, words such as *various, dozens* or *scores* may be used instead:

> *53 employees opted for voluntary redundancy.*

> *Dozens of employees opted for voluntary redundancy.*

few	less than expected
a few	approximately 3–6 depending on context
several	approximately 3–4
various	approximately 4–6
dozens of	approximately 30–60
scores of	approximately 60–100

■   Rewrite the following sentences using one of the words or phrases in the table above.

Example: (a) Only three people attended the meeting.
                            Few people attended the meeting.

(b) 77 students applied for the scholarship.

(c) He rewrote the essay three times.

(d) 54 books were published on the economic crisis.

(e) Five names were suggested, but rejected, for the new chocolate bar.

4 Further numerical phrases

The expressions listed below can also be used to present and simplify statistical information. For example:

The price of coffee rose from $750 to $1,550 in two years.

could be written:

The price of coffee doubled in two years.

If appropriate, *roughly/approximately* can be added:

The price of coffee roughly doubled in two years.

one in three	**One in three** new businesses ceases trading within a year.
twice/three times as many	**Twice as many** women as men study business law.
a five/tenfold increase	There was a **fivefold increase** in the price of oil.
to double/halve	The rate of inflation **halved** after 2008.
the highest/lowest	**The lowest** rate of home ownership was in Germany.
a quarter/fifth	**A fifth** of all employees leave every year.
the majority/minority	**The majority** of shareholders supported the board.
on average/the average	**On average**, each salesperson sells four cars a week.
a small/large proportion	The website generates **a large proportion of** their sales.

NB: 5–20% = a tiny/small minority
      40–49% = a substantial/significant minority
      51–55% = a small majority
      80%+ = a vast majority

■ Rewrite each sentence in a simpler way, using a suitable expression from the list above.

(a) In 1975, a litre of petrol cost 12p, while the price is now £1.20.

(b) Out of 18 students in the group, 12 were Japanese.

(c) The new high-speed train reduced the journey time to Madrid from seven hours to three hours 20 minutes.

(d) The number of students applying for the Management course has risen from 350 last year to 525 this year.

(e) Visitor numbers to the theme park show a steady increase. In 2012, there were 40,000 admissions, in 2013 82,000 and 171,000 in 2014.

(f) More than 80% of British students complete their first degree course; in Italy the figure is just 35%.

(g) Tap water costs 0.07p per litre while bottled water costs, on average, 50p per litre.

(h) The rate of unemployment ranges from 24% in Spain to 3% in Norway.

(i) 27 out of every hundred garments produced had some kind of fault.

(j) 57% of shareholders supported the proposal, but 83% of these expressed some doubts.

5 Practice

■ The following data were collected about a group of 15 international students. Write sentences about the group using the data.

Mother tongue		Future course		Age		Favourite sport	
Arabic	2	Accounting	1	21	1	Climbing	2
Chinese	8	Economics	3	22	3	Cycling	1
French	1	Finance	2	23	9	Dancing	3
Japanese	1	Management	6	24	–	Football	3
Korean	2	MBA	2	25	–	Swimming	5
Spanish	1	Tourism	1	26	1	Tennis	1

(a) *Roughly half the group speak Chinese.*

(b) _____

(c) _____

(d) _____

(e) _____

(f) _____

■ Write a few sentences about the students in your class.

UNIT 3.7 Prefixes and Suffixes

Prefixes and suffixes are the first and last parts of certain words. Understanding the meaning of prefixes and suffixes can help you work out the meaning of a word, and is particularly useful when you meet specialist new vocabulary.

1 How prefixes and suffixes work

'Unsustainable' is an example of a word containing a prefix and suffix. Words such as this are much easier to understand if you know how prefixes and suffixes affect word meaning.

Prefixes change or give the meaning.

Suffixes show the meaning or the word class (e.g. noun, verb).

Prefix	Meaning	STEM	Suffix	Word class/Meaning
un-	negative	**sustain**	**-able**	adjective/ability

The rate of growth was unsustainable (i.e. could not be continued).

2 Prefixes

(a) Negative prefixes: NON-, UN-, IN-, IM-, MIS-, DE- and DIS- often give nouns, adjectives and verbs a negative meaning: **non**sense, **un**clear, **in**capable, **im**possible, **mis**hear, **de**crease, **dis**agree.
(b) A wide variety of prefixes define meaning (e.g. PRE- usually means 'before'), hence **pre**fer, **pre**history and, of course, **pre**fix!

Common prefixes of meaning

■ Find the meaning(s) of each prefix. (NB: Some prefixes have more than one meaning.)

Prefix	Example	Example	Meaning
anti	antibiotic	Effective **antibiotics** were developed in 1942.	*against*
auto	automatically	Over-18s **automatically** have the right to vote.	
co	coordinator	The **coordinator** invited them to a meeting.	
ex	ex-president	The **ex-president** gave a speech on technology.	
ex	exclusive	It is difficult to join such an **exclusive** club.	
fore	forecast	The long-term **forecast** is for higher inflation.	
inter	intervention	Government **intervention** in the market is needed.	
macro	macroeconomics	Keynes focused on **macroeconomics**.	
micro	microscope	She examined the tiny animals with a **microscope**.	
multi	multinational	Ford is a **multinational** motor company.	
over	oversleep	He missed the lecture as he **overslept**.	
poly	polyglot	She was a true **polyglot**, speaking five languages.	
post	postpone	The meeting is **postponed** until next Monday.	
re	retrain	The firm **retrained** staff to use the new software.	
sub	subprime	**Subprime** mortgages led to the property market crash.	
trans	transmitter	Early radio **transmitters** were short-range.	
under	undergraduate	Most **undergraduate** courses last three years.	
under	undervalue	Buying **undervalued** assets can be profitable.	

3 Practice A

Prefixes allow new words to be created (e.g. 'unfriend' – to delete a 'friend' from social media).

■ **Suggest possible meanings for the recently developed words in bold.**

(a) Criminal activity seems to be very common among the **underclass**.

(b) The passengers found the plane was **overbooked** and had to wait for the next flight.

(c) The **microclimate** in this district allows early vegetables to be grown.

(d) It is claimed that information technology has created a **post-industrial** economy.

(e) Most film stars have **ex-directory** phone numbers.

(f) The class was **underwhelmed** by the quality of the lecture.

4 Suffixes

(a) Some suffixes such as -ION, -IVE or -LY help the reader find the word class (e.g. noun, verb or adjective)

(b) Other suffixes add to meaning (e.g. -FUL or -LESS after an adjective have a positive or negative effect – thought**ful**/care**less**).

Word class suffixes

Nouns	-ER often indicates a person: *teacher, gardener*
	-EE can show a person who is the subject: *employee, trainee*
	-ISM and -IST are often used with belief systems and their supporters: *socialism/socialist*
	-NESS converts an adjective into a noun: *sad/sadness*
	-ION changes a verb to a noun: *convert/conversion*
Adjectives	-IVE: *effective, constructive*
	-AL: *commercial, agricultural*
	-IOUS: *precious, serious*
Verbs	-ISE/-IZE to form verbs from adjectives: *private/privatise*
	NB: In the USA, only -IZE spelling is used, but both forms are accepted in the UK
Adverbs	-LY most (but not all) adverbs have this suffix: *happily*

Meaning suffixes

A few suffixes contribute to the meaning of the word:

-ABLE has the meaning of 'ability': *a profitable product, variable prices*

-WARDS means 'in the direction of': *the ship sailed northwards*

-FUL and –LESS: *hopeful news, a leaderless team*

5 Practice B

■ **Give the word class and suggest possible meanings for:**

(a) cancellation

(b) coincidental

(c) uncooperatively

(d) evolutionary

(e) protester

(f) unpredictable

(g) saleable

(h) interviewee

(i) consumerism

(j) symbolically

6 Practice C

■ **Study each sentence and find the meaning of the words underlined.**

(a) The film is an Anglo-Italian co-production made by a subsidiary company.

(b) When the car crashed, she screamed involuntarily but was unharmed.

(c) Using rechargeable batteries has undoubted benefits for the environment.

(d) The unavailability of the product is due to the exceptional weather.

(e) The miscommunication led to a reorganisation of their software system.

▶ **See Unit 3.3 Academic Vocabulary: Nouns and Adjectives**

Prepositions

Prepositions are generally short words such as 'by' or 'at', which have a variety of uses. They are important because different prepositions can change the meaning of a sentence. This unit explains how they can be understood, linking them to nouns, adjectives and verbs. Students should consult a standard English grammar for a full list of prepositional combinations.

1 Using prepositions

■ Underline the prepositions in the following text (ignoring to + infinitives).

The purpose of this paper is to examine the development of the textile industry in Catalonia over the period 1780–1880. This clearly contributed to the region's industrialisation, and was valuable for stimulating exports. In conclusion, the paper sets out to demonstrate the relationship between the decline in agricultural employment and the supply of cheap labour in the factory context.

■ The table lists the main ways of using prepositions. Find one example of each in the text.

Noun + preposition	*purpose of*
Verb + proposition	
Adjective + proposition	
Phrasal verb	
Preposition of place	
Preposition of time	
Phrase	

Note the difference between phrasal verbs and verbs with prepositions:

> *The cars are **made in** Korea.* (verb + preposition = easy to understand)

> *The researcher **made up** some of his data.* (phrasal verb = harder to understand)

2 Practice A

■ Study these further examples of preposition use and decide on their type.

(a) There are a number **of** limitations to be considered. (___*noun +*___)

(b) The results would be applicable **to** all employees. (_____)

(c) The data were gathered **from** a questionnaire. (_____)

(d) All the items were placed **within** their categories. (_____)

(e) The results **of** the investigation are still pertinent. (_____)

(f) The respondents had spent **on** average 4.9 years . . . (_____)

(g) Most countries **in** sub-Saharan Africa . . . (_____)

(h) **Within** a short spell of four years he had (_____)

3 Prepositions and nouns

■ Insert a suitable preposition in the sentences below.

(a) Evidence is presented in support _____ the value of women's work.

(b) A small change _____ demand can lead to large price fluctuations.

(c) Many examples _____ tax evasion were found.

(d) The answer _____ the problem was to retrain the workforce.

(e) Globalisation, _____ a political sense, involves a loss of national authority.

(f) The second point is their impact _____ developing countries.

4 Prepositions in phrases

■ Complete the following phrases with the correct preposition.

(a) _____the whole

(b) point _____ view

(c) in respect _____

(d) _____ spite of

(e) _____ conclusion

(f) _____ the other hand

(g) _____ order to

(h) standard _____ living

5 Prepositions of place and time

Note the difference between 'among' and 'between':

> *Among 14 students in the class, only two were from Africa.* (large group)

> *He divided his time between the offices in Barcelona and Madrid.* (limited number)

■ Complete the following sentences with suitable prepositions of place or time.

(a) _____ the respondents, few had any experience of working abroad.

(b) Industrial production declined gradually   1976   1985.

(c) Most workers _____ the European Union retire before the age _____ 60.

(d) Adam Smith was born _____ Scotland _____ 1723.

(e) Chocolate sales fall _____ summer and peak _____ Christmas.

(f) _____ the surface, there is no difference _____ male and female responses.

(g) The countries _____ the Mediterranean held a meeting _____ 20 May.

6 Practice B

■ Complete the following text with suitable prepositions.

This study sets (a) _____ to answer the controversial question
(b) _____ whether increased food supply (c) _____ a country
makes a significant contribution (d) _____ reducing malnutrition
(e) _____ children. It uses data collected (f) _____ 75 countries
(g) _____ 1995 and 2005. The findings are that there was a considerable
improvement (h) _____ the majority (i) _____ countries, despite
increases in population (j) _____ the period. However, a clear distinction
was found (k) _____ the poorest countries (e.g. (l) _____ South
Asia), where the improvement was greatest, and the wealthier states such as
those (m) _____ North Africa. Other factors, notably the educational level
(n) _____ women, were also found to be critical (o) _____
improving childhood nutrition.

7 Verbs and prepositions

The following verbs are generally used with these prepositions:

Verb + prep.	Example
add to	The bad weather **added to** the team's difficulties.
agree with	Yu (1997) **agrees with** Martin and Jenks (1989).
associate with	Monetarism is an economic policy **associated with** Mrs Thatcher.
believe in	The survey showed that 65% **believed in** Keynesian theory.
blame for	He **blamed** unfair questions **for** his poor exam results.
concentrate on (also: focus on)	She dropped all her hobbies to **concentrate on** her work.
consist of	The course **consists of** two parts: work experience and lectures.

Verb + prep.	Example
depend on (also: rely on)	The company **depends on** IT for a rapid flow of sales data.
derive from	Modern computers **derive from** wartime decoding machines
divide into	Trees are **divided into** two main types: conifers and deciduous.
invest in	Far more money needs to be **invested in** training programmes.
learn from	All successful students **learn from** their mistakes.
pay for	Goods delivered in April must be **paid for** by 30 June.
point out	Goodson (2001) **points out** the dangers of overgeneralisation.
specialise in	This department **specialises in** marine insurance.

8 Practice C

■ Complete the following with suitable verbs and prepositions.

(a) The enquiry _____ the cause of the accident, not the consequences.

(b) Dr Cracknell _____ that there were only two weeks before the deadline.

(c) Fewer British students are _____ foreign languages.

(d) The theory of relativity will always be _____ Albert Einstein.

(e) A football game is _____ two halves.

(f) A series of strikes were _____ the decline in production during May.

(g) Millions of men died for the cause they _____.

Synonyms

Synonyms are different words with a similar meaning. A good writer uses them to avoid repetition and thus provide more interest for the reader. Synonyms should also be used when paraphrasing or note-making to avoid plagiarism.

1 How synonyms work

■ Underline the synonyms in the following text and complete the table.

Royal Dutch Shell is the <u>largest</u> oil company in the world by revenue, with a significant share of the global hydrocarbon market. The <u>giant</u> firm employs over 90,000 people internationally, including over 8,000 employees in Britain.

Word/phrase	Synonym
largest	*giant*
oil	
company	
in the world	
people	

(a) Synonyms are not always exactly the same in meaning, and it is important not to change the register. 'Firm' is a good synonym for 'company', but 'boss' is too informal to use for 'manager'.

(b) Many common words (e.g. 'culture', 'economy' or 'industry') have no effective synonyms.

(c) The table below shows that although 'enterprise' can be a synonym for 'business', it is not a good synonym for 'corporation'.

Word	Application
firm	general
company	general
business	general
enterprise	used mainly for new and smaller businesses
corporation	used with larger companies

2 Common synonyms in academic writing

■ Match the synonyms in each list.

Nouns		Verbs	
area	advantage	accelerate	change
authority	part	alter	help
behaviour	argument	analyse	question
benefit	disadvantage	assist	explain
category	tendency	attach	evolve
component	**field**	challenge	examine
controversy	source	clarify	establish
drawback	emotion	concentrate on	insist
expansion	target	confine	speed up
feeling	explanation	develop	take apart
framework	conduct	evaluate	join
goal	topic	found	decrease
interpretation	possibility	maintain	demonstrate
issue	production	predict	increase
method	research	prohibit	cite
option	increase	quote	reinforce
quotation	citation	raise	focus on
results	figures	reduce	forecast
statistics	type	respond	ban
study	structure	retain	limit
trend	system	show	keep
output	findings	strengthen	reply

NB: These pairs are commonly synonymous, but not in every situation.

3 Practice A

■ Find synonyms for the words and phrases underlined, rewriting the sentences where necessary.

(a) Professor Hicks <u>questioned</u> the <u>findings</u> of the <u>research</u>.

(b) The <u>statistics show</u> a steady <u>increase</u> in student numbers.

(c) The institute's <u>prediction</u> has caused a major <u>controversy</u>.

(d) Cost seems to be the <u>leading drawback</u> to that <u>system</u>.

(e) They will <u>concentrate on</u> the first <u>option</u>.

(f) During the lecture, she tried to <u>clarify</u> her <u>concept</u>.

(g) Three <u>issues</u> need to be <u>examined</u>.

(h) The <u>framework</u> can be <u>retained</u> but the <u>goal</u> needs to be <u>altered</u>.

(i)   OPEC, the oil producers' cartel, is to <u>cut production</u> to <u>raise</u> global prices.

(j) The <u>trend</u> to smaller families has <u>speeded up</u> in the last decade.

4 Practice B

■ Identify the synonyms in this text by underlining them and linking them to the word they are substituting for.

Example: agency – organisation

The chairman of the UK's food standards <u>agency</u> has said that a national advertising campaign is necessary to raise low levels of personal hygiene. The <u>organisation</u> is planning a £3m publicity programme to improve British eating habits. A survey has shown that half the population do not wash before eating, and one in five fail to wash before preparing food. There are over 6 million cases of food poisoning in this country every year, and the advertising blitz aims to cut this by 20%. This reduction, the food body believes, could be achieved by regular hand washing prior to meals.

5 Practice C

■ In the following text, replace all the words or phrases in bold type with suitable synonyms.

Many motor manufacturers are currently introducing electric cars. Their aim is to **manufacture cars** which are cheaper to run and less polluting. But these **motor manufacturers** face several key difficulties. One **key difficulty** is the limited range of the battery, while another **difficulty** is its cost and weight. But the **motor manufacturers** predict that these **difficulties** will soon be overcome and **predict** that 10% of cars will be powered by electricity in five years' time.

Time Markers

Words such as 'during' and 'since' are often used to explain the timing of events. But the application of some of these words is restricted to particular tenses. This unit explains and practises their use.

1 How time markers are used

■ Study the following:

*She went on a training course **for** six weeks.* (with numbers, without start date)

*The report must be finished **by** 12 June.* (on or before)

*He has been president **since** 2007.* (with present perfect, must specify start date)

*They are studying in Bristol **until** March.* (end of a period)

*The library was opened two years **ago**.* (usually with past)

*The hotel is closed **during** the winter.* (with noun)

***Before** writing, he studied over 100 sources.* (often followed by -ing form; also **after**)

*He applied in May and was accepted two months **later**.* (often used with numbers; also **earlier**)

2 Tenses

■ Compare the tenses used with the following time markers:

Last year, there **was** an election in Spain. (past – finished event)

In the last year, there **has been** a decline in inflation. (present perfect – unfinished)

Recently, there **has been** a sharp rise in internet use. (present perfect – unfinished)

Currently, there **is** widespread concern about plagiarism. (present – focus on now)

3 Practice A

■ Choose the best alternative in each case.

(a) <u>Currently/Recently</u>, she has been researching the life cycle of SMEs.

(b) He worked there <u>until/during</u> he retired.

(c) Dr Hoffman has lived in Melbourne <u>since/for</u> 16 years.

(d) <u>Last month/In the last month</u>, a new book was published on banking.

(e) Applications must be received <u>by/on</u> 25 November.

(f) <u>Since/During</u> her arrival last May, she has reorganised the department.

(g) <u>During/For</u> the winter, most farmers in the region find work in the towns.

4 Practice B

■ Study the schedule for Professor Wang's recent trip and complete the sentences below with a suitable time marker. It is now 16 April.

12 March	Fly London – Barcelona
13–14 March	Conference in Barcelona
15 March	Train Barcelona – Paris
16 March	Lecture visit to Sorbonne
17 March	Fly Paris – Shanghai
18–19 March	Meeting with colleagues
20 March	Fly Shanghai – London

(a) _____ month, Professor Wang made a lengthy trip.

(b) _____her trip, she visited three countries.

(c) _____18 March, she had travelled 11,000 kilometres.

(d) She was away from home _____ nine days altogether.

(e) A month _____, she was in Paris.

(f) Two days _____, she was in Shanghai.

(g) She stayed in Shanghai _____ 20 March.

(h) _____ she is writing a report on her trip.

5 Practice C

■ Complete each gap in the following text with a suitable time marker.

Eating out

(a) _____ the last few decades there has been a significant change in eating habits in the UK. (b) _____ the early 1980s eating out in restaurants and cafes has increased steadily. There are several reasons for this trend.

50 years (c) _____ most women were housewives, and cooked for their families every day. But (d) _____, with more women working outside the home, less time has been available for food preparation. (e) _____, 71% of women aged 20–45 are at work, and (f) _____ 2020 it is estimated that this will rise to 85%.

Another factor is the growth in disposable income, which has risen significantly (g) _____ the late 1970s. With more money in their pockets people are more likely to save the trouble of shopping and cooking by visiting their local restaurant.

---

6 Practice D

■ Study the details of Henry Ford's life, and complete the biography below with suitable time markers (one word per gap).

1863   Born on a farm near Detroit, USA.
1879   Left home to work as a machinist.
1888   Married Clara Bryant and worked the family farm.
1893   Became Chief Engineer with the Edison company. Began to experiment with petrol engines.
1903   The Ford Motor Company was formed to build the car that he had designed.
1908   The Model T was introduced at a price of $825. It was successful because it was easily maintained and simple to drive.
1909   The price of the Model T was regularly reduced and sales climbed sharply.
1914   Ford shocked the industry by increasing wages to $5 a day. This successfully reduced labour turnover and attracted the best engineers to the company.
1916   The price of the Model T was cut to $360 and sales reached 472,000 annually.
1927   Production of the Model T was finally stopped after selling over 15 million. Sales had been declining for years, and it was replaced by the Model A.
1941   After years of conflict with the labour unions, Ford finally recognised the Union of Automobile Workers.
1945   Having kept effective control of the company into his 80s, he allowed his grandson, Henry Ford II, to become president.
1947   Henry Ford died at the age of 83.

Henry Ford

Henry Ford was born on a farm near Detroit and lived there (a) _____ he was 16. He returned to the farm nine years (b) _____ to marry Clara Bryant. However, he was more interested in machinery than farming and (c) _____ a few years he became an engineer with the Edison company, working there until 1899. (d) _____ this period he experimented with petrol engines and eventually built a car. (e) _____ 1903 he was confident enough to form a manufacturing company to produce cheap vehicles. The Model T, introduced in 1908, dominated the American market (f) _____ the next twenty years. Although Ford had been one of the leading American car makers (g) _____ the 1920s, unions were only recognised in 1941, (h) _____ a long struggle. Henry Ford retained control of his company (i) _____ old age, though (j) _____ his death he allowed his grandson to take over.

Writing Models

Case Studies

Both essays and reports may include case studies, which are detailed examples. One case study may be the main subject of a paper, or several may be included to illustrate different situations.

1 Using case studies

A case study attempts to show exactly what happened in a particular situation. For example, if you are studying microfinance, you might look at the performance of one specific scheme in a district of Dhaka in Bangladesh.

What are the advantages of including case studies?

Is there a disadvantage?

■ Match the topics on the left with the case studies on the right.

Topics	Case studies
Improving crop yields in semi-deserts	The Berlin experiment: increasing public participation in collecting and sorting waste
Encouraging entrepreneurship in Africa	The effect of the 2008 property crash on Spanish banking
Improving recycling rates in large cities	A study of a French supermarket training programme
The impact of the housing market on the wider economy	Using the internet to reduce visits to the doctor in Dublin
Approaches to motivation in the service sector	A Moroccan scheme for subsidising new business start-ups
Making health care more cost-effective	Using solar power to operate irrigation pumps in Ethiopia

2 Model case study

■ Read the following example and answer the questions below.

Topic: Adapting international brands to local markets

Case study: The experience of IKEA in China

Introduction

The Chinese economy has expanded at an annual rate of over 8% for the past 30 years. Parallel to this, the Chinese furniture industry has grown vigorously, with annual sales recently rising by over 20% a year. Legislation to privatise home ownership and rapidly rising income levels have created unprecedented growth in the home improvement market. According to estimates from the Credit Suisse group, China will be the world's second largest furniture market by 2014. This demand has boosted domestic production and also prompted international furniture manufacturers to enter this lucrative market.

IKEA, a Swedish furniture company, was one of the international companies to move into China. It is a major furniture retailer operating in over 40 countries around the world and has annual sales of over 21 billion euros (IKEA website). It entered the Chinese market in 1998 with its first store in Beijing, and sees great potential in the country, having already expanded to ten stores and five distribution centres. Despite this successful growth, IKEA has found itself facing a number of challenges in terms of local differences in culture and business practices.

Marketing IKEA in China

Marketing management needs to be largely tailored to local contexts. IKEA has kept this notion in mind when designing marketing strategies and trying to appeal to local customers while maintaining profitability. The company attempts to find the best possible compromise between standardisation and adaptation to the local markets. Its product policy pays careful attention to Chinese style and integrates the set of product attributes effectively (Armstrong and Kotler, 2006).

The store layouts reflect the floor plan of many Chinese apartments, and since many of these have balconies, the stores include a balcony section. In contrast with traditional Chinese furniture, which is dark with much carving, IKEA introduces a lighter and simpler style. However, efforts have been made to adapt its products to Chinese taste. For instance, it has released a series of products just before each Chinese New Year. In 2008, the year of the rat, the series 'Fabler' was designed, using the colour red which is associated with good luck.

Changes were also made to some product ranges. In Sweden, people are used to sleeping in single beds, or to putting two single beds together to form a double bed. However, this idea was not very well received by Chinese couples, due to the fact that sleeping in separate beds symbolises a poor relationship and is believed to bring bad luck. In addition, Chinese brand names should have positive connotations. The Chinese name of IKEA (Yi Jia) means 'comfortable home', which gives the company a useful advantage in the market.

An important feature of a retailer is the services it offers. The Shanghai store, for instance, has a children's playground and a large restaurant, which make it distinctive. However, Chinese consumers expect free delivery and installation, and although IKEA has reduced its charges for these, it still compares unfavourably with its competitors.

Price

When the company first entered China its target market was couples with an income of 5–8,000 Rmb per month. Following steady price reductions this has now been lowered to families with just over 3,000 Rmb. Various strategies have been adopted to achieve these reductions; the most effective being to source locally. 70% of its products sold in China are now made in the country (Song, 2005). Furthermore, IKEA replaced its thick, annual catalogue with thinner brochures which now appear five times a year. These not only cut printing costs but also give greater flexibility to adjust prices.

Accessibility is also an important issue for the Chinese market. In most countries IKEA stores are sited near main roads, but as only 20% of likely customers own cars in China, easy access to public transport is vital (Miller, 2004).

Advertising plays an important role in the total promotional mix. IKEA uses advertising effectively, with adverts in the local newspapers to keep customers informed of special offers. All TV commercials are produced locally with Chinese characters. Public relations is also vital to building a good corporate image. In China, IKEA co-operates with the Worldwide Fund for Nature (WWF) on forest projects. The company insists on using environmentally friendly and recyclable materials for the packaging of their products, as part of their efforts to build a good corporate image.

Discussion and conclusion

IKEA's product policy in China has been to successfully standardise products as much as possible, but also customise as much as needed. But it has learned that service is also vital: free delivery and installation are the perceived rules in the local market which it needs to follow. It has further found that it is better to locate in a downtown area, easily accessible with public transport, when free delivery is not provided. International companies which operate in China, such as IKEA, face more complicated marketing decisions than local companies. They must become culture-conscious and thoroughly research local requirements rather than simply introduce a standard model of business.

(a) What has IKEA done to adapt to the Chinese market?

(b) Give examples of problems the company has faced in this market.

(c) What could be done to improve the case study?

Formal Letters and Emails

Although less common than before electronic communication became available, letters are still important for formal matters, or when an email address is unknown. They are also considered to be more reliable than emails.

However, due to its convenience, email is increasingly used for semi-formal as well as informal communication. It is widely seen as a way of having a permanent record of an arrangement or discussion.

1 Letters

You have applied for a place on an MA course at a British university. On p. 218 is the letter you have received in reply.

■ Label the following features of formal letters with the letters (a–l) from the left margin.

(*d*) Date

(_____) Ending

(_____) Request for response

(_____) Greeting

(_____) Address of recipient

(_____) Address of sender

(_____) Further details

(a)   Central Admissions Office
                                        Wye House
                                       Park Campus
                                   University of Mercia
                                   Borchester BR3 5HT
                                     United Kingdom

(b) Ms P Tan
     54 Sydney Road
     Rowborough RB1 6FD

(c) Ref: MB/373

(d) 3rd May 2014

(e) Dear Ms Tan,

(f) **Application for MA Finance**

(g) Further to your recent application, I would like to invite you to the university for an informal interview on Tuesday 21st May at 11 am. You will be able to meet the course supervisor, Dr Schmidt, and look round the Business School.

(h) A map of the campus and instructions for finding the university are enclosed.

(i) Please let me know if you will be able to attend on the date given.

(j) Yours sincerely,

(k) *M. Bramble*

(l) Mick Bramble
     Administrative Assistant
     Central Admissions Office

     Enc.

(____) Reason for writing

(____) Sender's reference

(____) Subject headline

(____) Signature

(____) Writer's name and job title

Note the following points:

(a) The example opposite is addressed to a known individual and the ending is 'Yours sincerely'. However, when writing to somebody whose name you do not know (e.g. The Manager), use *Dear Sir* and *Yours faithfully*.

(b) A formal letter generally uses the family name in the greeting (*Dear Ms Tan*). Certain organisations may, however, use a first name with a family name or even a first name alone (*Dear Jane Tan, Dear Jane*).

(c) If the sender includes a reference, it is helpful to quote it in your reply.

■ **Write a reply to Mr Bramble making the following points:**

(a) You will attend the interview on the date given.

(b) You would like to have the interview one hour later, due to train times.

2 Emails

Starting and finishing

The following forms are acceptable ways to begin an email if you know the recipient:

  Hi Sophie, Dear Sophie, Hello Sophie

If you have not met the recipient, it may be safer to use:

  Dear Sophie Gratton, Dear Ms Gratton, Dear Dr Gratton

If you need to send an email to a large group (e.g. colleagues), you may use:

  Hi everyone, Hello all

In all cases, to close the message you can use:

  Regards, Best wishes, Best regards

You may also add a standard formula before this:

  Look forward to meeting next week, Let me know if you need further information

The main text

Here, you can use common contractions (I've, don't) and idiomatic language, but the normal rules for punctuation should be followed to avoid confusion. Spelling mistakes are just as likely to cause misunderstanding in emails as elsewhere. Always check for spelling and grammar problems before pressing the 'send' key. Note that emails tend to be short, although longer documents may be added as attachments.

3 Practice

■ Read the following and decide who the sender and recipient might be. Would Rachel expect a reply?

> Hello Dr Hoffman,
>
> I'm afraid I can't attend your Accounting Methods class this week, as I have to go for a job interview then. However, I will be there next Tuesday, when I am giving my paper (attached, as requested).
>
> See you then,
> Rachel

■ Write suitable emails for the following situations:

(a) You are writing to Mark, a colleague at work, to ask him to suggest a time to meet you tomorrow.

(b) Write to your teacher, Tricia James, to ask her to recommend another book for your current essay.

(c) Write to a group of classmates asking them how they want to celebrate the end of the course.

(d) Write an email in response to the one below. You have never had this book.

> According to our records, the copy of *Macroeconomics Today* you borrowed from the library on 12 October is now overdue. Your fine is currently £2.15. Please arrange to return this book as soon as possible.
>
> Best wishes,
> Tim Carey
> Library services

UNIT 4.3

Literature Reviews

> Literature reviews are sections of a paper in which the writer summarises recently published work on the topic. They are standard in dissertations, but in many essays a summary of relevant and recent authorities is included in the introduction.

1 Literature reviews

Occasionally, the whole focus of an essay may be a lengthy literature review, but in most student writing it will only form a relatively short section of the paper. Only a minority have a separate section headed 'The Literature' or 'Literature Review'. But in all cases, it is necessary to show that you are familiar with the main sources, so that your writing can build on these.

A literature review is not simply a list of sources that you have studied. It can be used to show that there is a gap in the research that your work attempts to fill:

> *This article has a different standpoint from other studies, because it believes that the influence of the state on the market has structurally increased since the neo-liberal era.*

> *This article focuses on information production, not information accessibility. That is the difference between this research and previous studies . . .*

It is also common to use the literature section to clarify the varying positions held by other researchers:

> *The political competition literature comprises two main strands – voter monitoring and political survival.*

▶ **See Unit 1.8 Combining Sources**

2 Example literature review

■ Study the following example, from a student essay on motivation theory. Answer the questions that follow.

CONTENT AND PROCESS THEORIES

The various theories of motivation are usually divided into content theories and process theories. The former attempt to 'develop an understanding of fundamental human needs' (Cooper *et al.*, 1992: 20). Among the most significant are Maslow's hierarchy of needs theory, McClellan's achievement theory and Herzberg's two-factor theory. The process theories deal with the actual methods of motivating workers, and include the work of Vroom, Locke and Adams.

Content theories

Maslow's hierarchy of needs theory was first published in 1943 and envisages a pyramid of needs on five levels, each of which has to be satisfied before moving up to the next level. The first level is physiological needs such as food and drink, followed by security, love, esteem and self-fulfilment (Rollinson, 2005: 195–196). This theory was later revised by Alderfer, who reduced the needs to three: existence, relatedness and growth, and re-named it the ERG theory. In addition, he suggested that all three needs should be addressed simultaneously (Steers *et al.*, 2004: 381). McClelland had a slightly different emphasis when he argued that individuals were primarily motivated by three principal needs: for achievement, affiliation and power (Mullins, 2006: 1999).

In contrast, Herzberg suggested, on the basis of multiple interviews with engineers and accountants during the 1950s, a two-factor theory: that job satisfaction and dissatisfaction had differing roots. He claimed that so-called hygiene factors such as conditions and pay were likely to cause negative attitudes if inadequate, while positive attitudes came from the nature of the job itself. In other words, workers were satisfied if they found their work intrinsically interesting, but would not be motivated to work harder merely by good salaries or holiday allowances. Instead workers needed to be given more responsibility, more authority or more challenging tasks to perform (Vroom and Deci, 1992: 252). Herzberg's work has probably been the most influential of all the theories in this field, and is still widely used today, despite being the subject of some criticism, which will be considered later.

Process theories

Vroom's expectancy theory hypothesises a link between effort, performance and motivation. It is based on the idea that an employee believes that increased effort will result in improved performance. This requires a belief that the individual will be supported by the organisation in terms of training and resources (Mullins, 2006). In contrast, Locke emphasised the importance of setting clear targets to improve worker performance in his goal theory. Setting challenging but realistic goals is necessary for increasing employee motivation: 'goal specificity, goal difficulty and goal commitment each served to enhance task performance' (Steers *et al.*, 2004: 382). This theory has implications for the design and conduct of staff appraisal systems and for management by objective methods focusing on the achievement of agreed performance targets.

Another approach was developed by Adams in his theory of equity, based on the concept that people value fairness. He argued that employees appreciate being treated in a transparently equitable manner in comparison with other workers doing similar functions, and respond positively if this is made apparent (Mullins, 2006). This approach takes a wider view of the workplace situation than some other theories, and stresses the balance each worker calculates between 'inputs' i.e. the effort made, and 'outputs', which are the rewards obtained.

(a) How many types of motivation theory are described?

(b) How many different theorists are mentioned?

(c) How many sources are cited?

(d) Why has the writer not referred to the work of the theorists directly but used secondary sources instead?

UNIT 4.4 **Longer Essays**

> Long essays of 2,500–5,000 words may be required as part of a module assessment. These require more research and organisation than short essays, and this unit provides a guide to how such an assignment can be tackled.

Planning your work

Longer assignments are normally set many weeks before their deadline, which means that students should have plenty of time to organise their writing. However, it is worth remembering that at the end of a semester, you may have to complete several writing tasks, so it may be a good idea to finish one earlier.

You should also check the submission requirements of your department. These include style of referencing, method of submission (i.e. electronic, hard copy or both) and place and time of submission. Being clear about these will avoid last-minute panic.

(a) The first thing is to prepare a schedule for your work. An eight-week schedule might look like this:

Week	Stages of work	Relevant units in *Academic Writing for International Students of Business*
1	Study title and make first outline. Look for and evaluate suitable sources.	1.4
2	Reading and note-making. Keep record of all sources used.	1.2, 1.3, 1.5, 1.6
3	Reading, note-making, paraphrasing and summarising. Modify outline.	1.2, 1.3, 1.5, 1.6
4	Write draft of main body.	1.8, 1.9
5	Write draft introduction and conclusion.	1.10
6	Rewrite introduction, main body and conclusion, checking for logical development of ideas and relevance to title.	1.11
7	Organise list of references, contents, list of figures and appendices if required. Check all in-text citations.	1.7
8	Proofread the whole essay before handing it in. Make sure that the overall presentation is clear and accurate.	1.11

(b) How you actually plan your schedule is up to you, but the important thing is to organise your time effectively. Leaving the writing stage until the last minute will not lead to a good mark, however much research you have done. Although you may be tempted to postpone writing, the sooner you start, the sooner you will be able to begin refining your ideas. Remember that late submission of coursework is usually penalised.

(c) Longer papers may include the following features, in this order:

Title page	Apart from the title, this usually shows the student's name and the module title and number.
Contents page	This should show the reader the basic organisation of the essay, with page numbers.
List of tables or figures	If the essay includes visual features such as graphs, these need to be listed by title and page number.
Introduction	
Main body	If a numbering system is used, the chief sections of the main body are normally numbered 1, 2, 3 and then subdivided 1.1, 1.2, etc.
Conclusion	
List of references	This is a complete list of all the sources cited in the text. Writers occasionally also include a bibliography, which is a list of sources read but not cited.
Appendices (singular – appendix)	These sections are for data related to the topic that the reader may want to refer to. Each appendix should have a title and be mentioned in the main body.

UNIT
4.5

Reports

Although essays are the most common assignments in many academic disciplines, students of Economics and Business are often asked to write reports. Reports and essays are similar in many ways, but this unit explains and illustrates the differences.

1 Writing reports

While essays are often concerned with abstract or theoretical subjects, a report is a description of a situation or something that has happened. In academic terms, it might describe a survey you have carried out or be a comparison of alternative proposals to deal with a situation.

Reports may include some or all of the following components:

Introduction
- background to the subject
- reasons for carrying out the work
- review of other research in the area.

Methods
- how you did your research
- description of the tools/materials used.

Results
- what you discovered
- comments on likely accuracy of results.

Discussion
- of your main findings
- comments on the effectiveness of your research.

Conclusion

- summary of your work
- suggestions for further research.

2 Essays and reports

In comparison with essays, reports are likely to:

(a) be based on primary as well as secondary research
(b) use numbering (1.1, 1.2) and subheadings for different sections
(c) be more specific and detailed

In most other respects, reports are similar to essays, since both:

(a) have a clear and logical format
(b) use objective and accurate academic style
(c) include citations and references
(d) make use of visual information in the form of graphs and tables
(e) include appendices where necessary

■   **Decide whether the following topics are more likely to be written as reports or essays.**

Topic	Report	Essay
1. The development of trade unions in South Africa and their role in the future		
2. A study of a struggling retail business and proposals to improve its performance		
3. A study you conducted to compare male and female attitudes to buying fresh food		
4. A review of recent research on farming co-operatives in Thailand		
5. The macroeconomic consequences of negative interest rates		

▶   **For an example of report writing, see Unit 4.6 Surveys**

3 Practice

The plans below illustrate two proposals for redeveloping a site on a university campus.

■ Study the plans and then read the five sentences (a–e) that are the introduction to a report on the redevelopment. The order of the sentences has been mixed up. Put them in the correct order. Then write the rest of the report in about 250 words.

Plan A

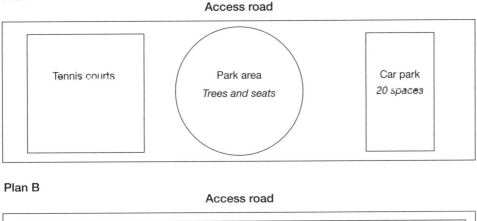

Plan B

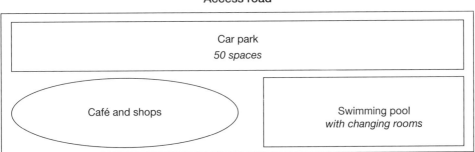

(a) The report takes into account a consultation exercise with staff and students carried out last autumn.

(b) Two alternatives schemes for redevelopment have been put forward, as can be seen in Plans A and B above.

(c) This report attempts to compare the two schemes on this basis and to establish which is the more suitable.

(d) The aim of the redevelopment is to improve facilities for both staff and students, and at the same time enhance the appearance of this part of the campus.

(e) Due to the recent closure of the maintenance depot, a site approximately 250 metres long and 100 metres wide has become vacant on the west side of the university campus.

UNIT 4.6 **Surveys**

> Surveys, in which people are asked questions about their behaviour or opinions, are a common feature of academic work. This unit deals with the design of effective questionnaires for surveys, and presents a suitable structure for reporting the results.
>
> Note that these questionnaires are designed to collect data from large numbers of people fairly quickly. Another research method uses a longer interview for a more detailed response; this is not dealt with here.

1 Conducting surveys

What are the reasons for carrying out surveys in academic life?

■ **List your ideas below.**

(a) *To replicate other research*

(b) _____

(c) _____

(d) _____

2 Questionnaire design

Writing an effective series of questions is a vital part of conducting a survey. You must think carefully about what your aims are, and how to achieve them in the simplest way. There is no value in collecting a mass of information that is irrelevant to your topic.

(a) Which is the better question?

    (i) *How old are you?*

    (ii) *Are you (a) under 20 (b) between 21 and 30 (c) over 30?*

(b) What is the main difference between the two questions below?

    (i) *How do you usually relax at weekends?*

    (ii) *At weekends, do you relax by (a) doing sport (b) playing computer games (c) sleeping?*

(c) How many questions should your questionnaire contain?

When designing your questionnaire:

(a) Limit the number of questions so the respondent can answer them in a minute or two. Long and complicated questionnaires will not receive accurate replies.

(b) Keep questions clear and simple, and not too personal.

(c) Closed questions (b(ii)) are easier to process, but open questions (b(i)) will collect a wider range of responses.

(d) You should try putting the questions to a classmate before beginning the full survey, and be ready to modify any that were not clear.

(e) Do not collect unnecessary information (e.g. Do you need to know if the respondent is undergraduate or postgraduate? If not, don't ask!).

3 Survey language

■ Study the report of a survey carried out on a university campus.
Complete the report by inserting suitable words from the box below into the gaps (more words than gaps).

sample	conducted	method	respondents	random	questions
majority	questioned	mentioned	interviewees	common	
questionnaire	unusual	generally	minority	slightly	

Student experience of part-time work

Introduction

With the introduction of course fees and the related increase in student debt, more students are finding it necessary to work part-time. The survey was (a) _____ to find out how this work affects student life and study.

Method

The research was done by asking students selected at (b) _____ on the campus to complete a (c) _____ (see Appendix 1). 50 students were (d) _____ on Saturday, 23 April, with approximately equal numbers of male and female students.

Table 1 Do you have, or have you had, a part-time job?

	Men	Women	Total	%
Have job now	8	7	15	30
Had job before	4	6	10	20
Never had job	14	11	25	50

Findings

Of the (e) _____, 30% currently had part-time jobs, 20% had had part-time jobs, but half had never done any work during university semesters (see Table 1). (f) _____ who were working or who had worked were next asked about their reasons for taking the jobs. The most common reason was lack of money (56%), but many students said that they found the work useful experience (32%) and others (g) _____ social benefits (12%).

The 25 students with work experience were next asked about the effects of the work on their studies. A significant (h) _____ (64%) claimed that there were no negative effects at all. However, 24% said that their academic work suffered (i) _____, while a small (j) _____ (12%) reported serious adverse results, such as tiredness in lectures and falling marks.

Further (k) _____ examined the nature of the work that the students did. The variety of jobs was surprising, from van driver to busker, but the most (l) _____ areas were catering and bar work (44%) and secretarial work (32%). Most students worked between 10 and 15 hours per week, though two (8%) worked over 25 hours. Rates of pay were (m) _____ near the national minimum wage, and averaged £6.80 per hour.

The final question invited students to comment on their experience of part-time work. Many (44%) made the point that students should be given larger grants so that they could concentrate on their studies full-time, but others felt that they gained something from the experience, such as meeting new people and getting insights into various work environments. One student said that she had met her current boyfriend while working in a city centre restaurant.

Conclusions

It is clear that part-time work is now a common aspect of student life. Many students find jobs at some point in their studies, but an overwhelming majority (88%) of those deny that it has a damaging effect on their studies. Most students work for only 2–3 hours per day on average, and a significant number claim some positive results from their employment. Obviously, our survey was limited to a relatively small (n) _____ by time constraints, and a fuller study might modify our findings in various ways.

4 Question forms

Question 1 is given in Table 1 on p. 232. What were the other questions asked in this survey?

■ Using the report, write possible questions below.

2 _____

3 _____

4 _____

5 _____

6 _____

7 _____

5 Tenses

What is the main tense in (a) Findings and (b) Conclusion?

■ Explain the reasons for the difference.

6 Practice

■ You are preparing a survey on one of the following subjects. Write a questionnaire of no more than six questions to collect the most useful data.

(a) Patterns of student spending

(b) Student satisfaction with teaching methods

(c) Customer attitudes to taxi companies

Revision Exercise
Taking Ideas from Sources

This exercise revises the process of note-making, paraphrasing, summarising and referencing introduced in Units 1.5–1.8, showing how a relevant source can be accurately incorporated into your work.

Can money buy happiness?

You have been told to write an essay on the title: *Can money buy happiness?*

You have found the following text, which seems relevant to this topic. It is part of an article by A. Penec in a journal called *Applied Econometrics* (volume 44, pp. 18–27) published in 2008.

■ Read it and underline the key points.

THE MEASUREMENT OF HAPPINESS

Economists have recently begun to pay more attention to studying happiness, instead of just using the more traditional measure of GDP per person. They have found that in the last fifty years there has been no apparent increase in personal happiness in Western nations, despite steadily growing economic wealth. In both Europe and the USA surveys have found no rise in the level of happiness since the

1950s, which seems surprising given that wealthier people generally claim to be happier than poorer people. In America, for example, more than a third of the richest group said they were 'very happy', while only half this proportion of the poorest made the same claim. Although it would be logical to expect that rising national wealth would lead to greater general happiness, this has not happened. Individually, more money does seem to increase happiness, but when the whole society becomes richer, individuals do not appear to feel better off.

One possible explanation has been that people rapidly get used to improvements, and therefore devalue them because they are taken for granted. Central heating is a good example: whereas 50 years ago it was a luxury item, today it is standard in nearly every home. Another theory is that the figures for GDP per person, used to assess national wealth, do not take into account quality of life factors such as environmental damage or levels of stress, which must affect people's feelings of happiness. The report of a commission set up by the French president recently claimed that the French were comparatively better off than had been previously thought, due to their generous holidays and effective health care system, factors which basic GDP figures had ignored.

(a) The text contains five key points:

(i)   Economists have recently begun to pay more attention to studying happiness, instead of just using the more traditional measure of GDP per person.
(ii) In the last fifty years there has been no apparent increase in personal happiness in Western nations, despite steadily growing economic wealth.
(iii) . . . which seems surprising given that wealthier people generally claim to be happier than poorer people.
(iv) One possible explanation has been that people rapidly get used to improvements, and therefore devalue them because they are taken for granted.
(v)   Another theory is that the figures for GDP per person, used to assess national wealth, do not take into account quality of life factors such as environmental damage or levels of stress . . .

(b) The next step is to make notes of these points, using paraphrase:

(i)   Economists have begun to research happiness, rather than rely on GDP.
(ii) Although W. economies have grown since 1950s, no parallel growth in happiness.
(iii) But more rich people than poor people say they are happy.
(iv) Apparently people soon get accustomed to gains, so don't appreciate them.
(v)   GDP does not measure environmental or social factors that affect individuals.

(c) These points can now be combined into one paragraph of your essay, using conjunctions where necessary, and including a reference to your source:

A recent development in economics is the study of personal happiness. Penec (2008) argues that although Western economies have grown since the 1950s, there has been no parallel growth in happiness. Surveys indicate that rich people generally say they are happier than poor people, but this does not transfer to the whole society. One explanation is that people soon become accustomed to gains and so do not appreciate them. It also seems likely that GDP measurement ignores significant social and environmental factors which affect personal well-being.

■ (d) Continue the same process with the next section of the text by underlining the key points.

A further explanation for the failure of wealth to increase happiness is the tendency for people to compare their own position to that of their neighbours. Studies show that people would prefer to have a lower income, if their colleagues got less, rather than a higher income while colleagues got more. In other words, happiness seems to depend on feeling better off than other people, rather than on any absolute measure of wealth. Further research suggests that having free time is also closely linked to happiness, so that the pattern of working harder in order to buy more goods is unlikely to increase well-being. Yet Western societies generally encourage employees to spend as much time at work as possible.

■ (e) Make notes on the key points.

(i) _____

(ii) _____

■ (f) Link the notes together and expand them to conclude this section of your essay.

■ (g) Write a full reference for the source as it would appear in the list of references.

Answers

Providing answers for a writing course is less clear-cut than for other language areas. In some exercises, there is only one possible answer, but in other cases several possibilities exist. Teachers need to use common sense, and accept any reasonable answer. In the case of exercises where students can choose their own topic and it is therefore impossible to provide an answer, students still appreciate having a model answer, and so some have been included.

Answers: Part 1

Academic writing quiz

1. b (see Unit 1.2)
2. c (see Unit 1.1)
3. a (see Unit 1.4)
4. c (see Unit 1.10)
5. b (see Unit 1.3)
6. c (see Unit 1.5)
7. a (see Unit 1.7)
8. b (see Unit 1.6)
9. c (see Unit 1.9)
10. a (see Unit 1.10)
11. b (see Unit 1.11)
12. c (see Unit 1.2)

1.1 Background to Writing

1 The purpose of academic writing

Other reasons might include:

- to present a hypothesis for consideration by others
- to make notes on something read or heard.

Possibilities include:

- semi-formal vocabulary, lack of idioms
- use of citation/references
- use of both passive and active.

2 Common types of academic writing

Notes: A written record of the main points of a text or lecture, for a student's personal use.
Report: A study of something that has happened (e.g. a survey a student has conducted)

Project: A piece of research, either individual or group work, with the topic chosen by the student(s).

Essay: The most common type of written work, with the title given by the teacher, normally 1,000–5,000 words.

Dissertation/Thesis: The longest piece of writing normally done by a student (20,000+ words) often for a higher degree, on a topic chosen by the student.

Paper: A general term for any academic essay, report or article.

3 The format of long and short writing tasks

(a) abstract
(b) references
(c) appendix
(d) acknowledgements
(e) literature review
(f) case study

4 The format of academic writing

(a) title
(b) subtitle
(c) heading
(d) phrase
(e) sentence
(f) paragraph

6 Simple and longer sentences

Model sentences:

(a) In 2011, the company produced nearly 165,000 vehicles.
(b) Vehicle production fell in 2012.
(c) Vehicle production declined slightly in 2012, and then more steeply in 2013.
(d) Between 2009 and 2013, vehicle production peaked in 2011, when the number reached over 164,000.

7 Writing in paragraphs

▶   See Unit 1.9 Organising Paragraphs

Paragraph 2 begins: The first issue to . . .
Paragraph 3 begins: Diversification must also . . .
Paragraph 4 begins: A further consideration . . .

1.2 Critical Reading

1 Academic texts

Text 1: Yes, it summarises some relevant research and includes citations.
Text 2: No, it is apparently an informal personal report.
Text 3: Possibly, it appears to be a newspaper article.
Text 4: Yes, it is apparently an academic article.

Possible answers:

Feature	Example
1 Formal vocabulary	. . . the marketing planning process in tourism marketing . . .
	. . . the extent of political-economic dependency . . .
2 Use of citation	(Buckley and Witt, 1990; Hall, 1991)
3 Impersonal style	. . . it has also long been recognised that . . .
	. . . it is important to study the tourists' attitude . . .
4 Long, complex sentences	Equally, from a political perspective, the nature of state involvement in and policies for tourism is dependent on both the political-economic structures and the prevailing political ideology in the destination state, with comparisons typically made between market-led and centrally planned economies.

2 Types of text

Possible answers:

Text type	Advantage	Disadvantage
Textbook	Written for students	May be too general or outdated
Website	Usually up to date	Possibly unreliable and unedited
Journal article	Often focuses on a special area	May be too specialised or complex
Official report (e.g. from the government)	Contains a lot of detail	May not be objective
Newspaper or magazine article	Easy to read and up to date	May not be objective and not give sources
e-book	Easily accessible	Must be read on screen

4 Using library catalogues

Title 1 has a limited focus. Title 2 might be up to date, while Title 3 only looks at one area of exploration. Title 4 might provide a general picture. The remaining titles are unlikely to be useful.

6 Reading methods

<u>Choosing suitable texts</u>

```
┌─────────────────────────────────────────┐
│       Read title and sub-title carefully │
└─────────────────────────────────────────┘

┌─────────────────────────────────────────┐
│     Survey text features (e.g. abstract, │
│              contents, index)            │
└─────────────────────────────────────────┘

┌──────────────────────────┐  ┌──────────────────────────────┐
│ Skim text for gist – is   │  │  Scan text for information you │
│         it relevant?      │  │         need (e.g. names)      │
└──────────────────────────┘  └──────────────────────────────┘

┌─────────────────────────────────────────┐
│        Read extensively when             │
│        useful sections are found         │
└─────────────────────────────────────────┘

┌─────────────────────────────────────────┐
│      Read intensively to make notes      │
│              on key points               │
└─────────────────────────────────────────┘
```

Possible answers:

(a) Skimming is to find the main ideas
     Scanning aims to locate specific details

(b) Text genre recognition
     Dealing with new vocabulary

8 Assessing texts critically

1   Probably unreliable. The adjectives used (easily, quickly) and the lack of concrete information suggest that this text is not to be trusted.
2   Probably reliable. The advice the writer is giving appears common sense, although not everyone might agree with all of it (e.g. cooking is fun).
3   Probably reliable. The facts given can be confirmed by students' own experience.

Change on the farm
Positive: Current, relevant, some statistics
Negative: Lack of detail, no references, rather superficial

9 Critical thinking

The responses to these questions will vary from student to student, which is the nature of the critical approach.

10 Vocabulary revision

Stakeholders: All parties involved in a business
Productivity: A measure of a company's output per worker
Patent: Method of protecting new inventions from copying
Debt: Money owed
Commodity prices: Cost of raw materials such as wheat or oil
Workforce: Employees of an organisation
Budgeting: Process of planning future spending priorities
Privatisation: Process of selling state-owned assets
Bias: Preference for one point of view
Diversification: Spreading business activities over several areas

1.3 Avoiding Plagiarism

2 Degrees of plagiarism

1 Yes
2 Yes
3 Yes
4 No
5 Yes
6 No
7 Yes
8 No
9 Yes/No
10 Yes

3 Avoiding plagiarism by summarising and paraphrasing

(a) Acceptable –a correctly referenced summary
(b) Plagiarised – original wording with minor changes to word order
(c) Acceptable – a correctly referenced quotation
(d) Technically plagiarism – mistake in date means the citation is incorrect
(e) Plagiarised – some original wording and no citation

4 Avoiding plagiarism by developing good study habits

Possible further suggestions:

- Check that your quotations are exactly the same wording as the original.
- When paraphrasing, alter the structure as well as the vocabulary.

5 Vocabulary revision

Source: Any text that students use to obtain ideas or information
Citation: Short in-text note giving the author's name and publication date
Summarise: To reduce the length of a text but keeping the main points
Quotation: Using the exact words of the original text in your work
Reference: Full publication details of a text to allow a reader to access the original
To cheat: To gain advantage dishonestly

1.4 From Understanding Titles to Planning

2 Analysing essay titles

(a) Summarise/discuss
Asking for an analysis of the factors driving e-commerce, and a consideration of possible consequences.

(b) Critically evaluate
Asking for an examination of the impact of the internet on the standard theories of internationalisation.

(c) Describe/critically examine
Asking for an account of the problems faced by HRM in this area and an evaluation of how some companies deal with this.

(d) Discuss/Consider
Asking for an evaluation of some of the literature on these topics, and the impact these theories might have on management.

3 Practice: key words

Analyse: Break down into the various parts and their relationships
Assess/Evaluate: Decide the value or worth of a subject
Describe: Give a detailed account of something
Discuss: Look at various aspects of a topic, compare benefits and drawbacks
Examine/Explore: Divide into sections and discuss each critically/consider widely
Illustrate: Give examples
Outline/Trace: Explain a topic briefly and clearly
Suggest: Make a proposal and support it
Summarise: Deal with a complex topic by reducing it to the main elements

4 Brainstorming

Possible answer:

International Tourism – Segmentation of market

How and why

* Package holidays made foreign holidays popular in 1950s and 1960s
* In 1960s, jet aircraft permitted faster travel – long and short haul holidays
* In 1990s, budget airlines lowered costs – short breaks
* Now, internet allows travellers to plan own holidays

Economic forces

* Rising disposable incomes permit more spending on travel
* Developing countries see tourism as route to growth
* Older, retired people spend more on travel

5 Essay length

These figures are only a guide and individual students may have a different approach:

(a) Describe/How
Approximately 50:50

(b) Explain/Discuss
Approximately 30:70

(c) What/Discuss
Approximately 50:50

6 Outlines

(c) Lists are more logical, make it easier to allocate space, but are rather inflexible. Mind maps are more flexible as extra items can be added easily.

(d) *Possible outline:*

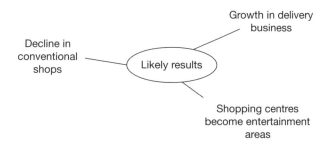

1.5 Finding Key Points and Note-making

1 Finding key points

Possible titles include:

Marketing to the older generation
Selling to retired people
An ageing market

Key points:
(a) The generation born after World War II, sometimes called the baby-boomers, are now reaching retirement age, and businesses are starting to realise that they are a wealthier market than any previous retirement group.
(b) There are, however, certain difficulties in selling to this market. Some customers resent being addressed as 'old' since they see themselves as more youthful, while there is a huge variation in the profile of the baby-boomers.

2 Finding relevant points

Key points:

(1) The practice of imposing taxes on products which are thought to have a negative social impact, such as alcohol, has been accepted for several hundred years . . .
(2) It has recently been suggested in the USA that so-called junk food should be taxed in order to compensate for the social costs of the obesity it is believed to cause. This proposal is based on the estimate of the medical costs of obesity, which is thought to be linked to cancer, diabetes and heart disease.
(3) A study of the long-term effects of changes in food prices (Goldman, Lakdawalla and Zheng, 2009) argues that significant changes in consumption, and hence obesity levels, can be achieved over the long-term.
(4) But the link between junk food and ill-health is not easily determined. A physically active person could eat hamburgers daily and still keep slim.
(5) It has even been suggested that such a 'fat tax' might have the opposite effect and reduce activity levels by forcing people to spend more time preparing food for themselves, instead of buying it from fast-food outlets (Yaniv, Rosin and Tobol, 2009).
(6) . . . other studies on the effects of alcohol and tobacco taxes indicate that the heaviest users of these products are the least influenced by price rises . . .

3 Practice A

Source: Rohan, J. (2010) *Public Health Review* 8, p. 36
<u>Taxing junk food</u>

(1) Goods > social harm (e.g. alcohol) have been taxed since 18th C
(2) US proposal to tax junk food > reduce obesity > cut medical costs (diabetes, heart disease)

(3) Goldman, Lakdawalla and Zheng (2009) claim that raising food prices can reduce consumption in long term
(4) No clear link health/junk food – active people stay thin
(5) Yaniv, Rosin and Tobol (2009) argue that tax on fast food might have undesired effect of making people cook more > cut their exercise time
(6) Research on tax on alcohol shows that main users are unaffected by increase in prices

4 Why make notes?

(a) To prepare for essay writing
(b) To avoid plagiarism
(c) To keep a record of reading/lectures
(d) To revise for exams
(e) To help remember main points

5 Note-making methods

The notes are paraphrased, not copied from the text.
The language is simplified and symbols are used.

7 Practice B

Source: Caballero J. and Poledna Z. (2010) *European Business Prospects*, London: University Press, p. 351

Predatory pricing (PP) = using size to lower prices below cost to harm competitors

In USA 1890 Sherman Antitrust Act – example of govt. attempt to control monopolies

But low prices benefit customers + predation hard to prove legally
   – good reasons for selling below cost (e.g. new product promotion)
   – bundling (selling several items together) makes proof harder (i.e. calculating individual profit margins)

Example: 5/09 EU fined Intel €1 bn. for PP against rival AMD – but very complex case and Intel appealed verdict

8 Vocabulary revision

(a) Something sold for money management (e.g. insurance policy, bond or credit card)
(b) Causing social damage (e.g. crime)
(c) Limiting demand
(d) Tax system that penalises poorer people
(e) Laws that aim to prevent one business controlling a market
(f) Attempt by large company to use its power to cut prices to damage competitors
(g) Forcing rival companies out of business

(h) Balancing a loss in one area with profits from others
(i) Demonstrate bad behaviour
(j) Number of copies sold per issue

1.6 Summarising and Paraphrasing

1 What makes a good summary?

A good summary: selection of most important aspects/clear description/accuracy

2 Stages of summarising

1 (c)
2 (d)
3 (b)
4 (a)
5 (e)

3 Practice A

1 (c)
2 (b)
3 (a)

4 Practice B

(b) *Model answers:*

(i) Falling levels of fertility have generally been found as countries become richer.
(ii) In some, number of children born fell below replacement rate.
(iii) Two results: smaller populations and larger numbers of elderly needing assistance.
(iv) Recent research claims that a new situation may be developing.
(v) Comparison of HDI (human development index) (life expectancy, income and education) with fertility found that in most highly rated (+0.9) countries, fertility is rising.

(c) *Model summary:*

Wealth and fertility

Falling levels of fertility have generally been found as countries become richer. In some, the number of children born has fallen below the replacement rate. There are two likely results: smaller populations and larger numbers of elderly needing assistance. But recent research claims that this pattern may be changing. A comparison of HDI (human development index) (life expectancy, income and education) with fertility found that in the most highly rated (HDI +0.9) countries, fertility is rising.

(d) *Model summary:*

Research suggests that the long-term decline in human fertility may be reversing in some of the most advanced societies.

5 Practice C

Model summary:

The Washlet is an expensive luxury lavatory that is popular in crowded Japanese homes, with a range of special features. Its maker, the Toto company, is hoping to expand sales in the West, but different regulations about toilet design and electrical fittings make this a challenging goal.

7 Practice D

(a) Quite good, but lack of precision (at that time) and unsuitable register (bosses)
(b) The best paraphrase, with all main points included and a significantly different structure
(c) A poor paraphrase, with only a few words changed and extra and inaccurate information added (Britain was the only country . . .)

9 Practice E

Model answer:

(a) It is <u>frequently claimed</u> that governments can create <u>jobs</u> and <u>cut</u> carbon emissions by investing in renewable energy <u>schemes</u>. These so-called 'green jobs' have the <u>attraction</u> of helping to <u>fight</u> global warming while <u>lowering</u> a <u>nation's</u> dependence on imported fuels.

(b) But there are <u>claims</u> by critics of these schemes that the <u>benefits</u> are less than they seem. Firstly, <u>spending</u> the money on other projects such as road-building would also allow the <u>creation</u> of jobs.

(c) Secondly, the taxpayer has to finance higher government borrowing to pay for the investment, and all business borrowing may eventually be affected. In addition, the price of electricity for consumers may be raised by subsidising solar and wind power, which are relatively inefficient sources of energy.

(d) A Spanish study examined potential subsidies given over 25 years to renewable energy. It found that each of the 50,000 jobs created cost €570,000, with an estimated total spending of €29 billion. But had the state permitted the same sum to be spent by private businesses they would have produced over twice as many jobs: 113,000. According to these calculations the subsidies in Spain have effectively eliminated more than 50,000 posts.

10 Vocabulary revision

(a) **Assess**: assessment
Economise: economy
Subsidise: subsidy
Impede: impediment
Translate: translation

(b) **Innovation**: innovate
Correlation: correlate
Replacement: replace
Installation: install
Mechanisation: mechanise
Dependence: depend

1.7 References and Quotations

1 Why use references?

(a) No
(b) Yes
(c) Yes
(d) No
(e) Yes
(f) No

2 Citations and references

(a) Friedman (1974)
(b) Friedman (1974: 93)

(a) is a summary and (b) a quotation

A summary is very flexible in terms of length. A quotation has the benefit of using the original words of the source, which can give authority.

5 Practice

Model answers:

(a) According to Hoffman (2009), mobile phones have a powerful impact in the developing world as they offer previously unavailable services, and have led to the growth of new, focused local operators.

(b) Hoffman points out that the special conditions in the developing world have produced new phone operators: 'that are larger and more flexible than Western companies, and which have grown by catering for poorer customers . . .' (Hoffman, 2009: 87).

(c) Hoffman (2009) argues that the impact of mobile telephony on developing countries is significant as they offer services previously unavailable, and has led to the growth of new local operators, which: 'are larger and more flexible than Western companies, and which have grown by catering for poorer customers . . .' (Hoffman, 2009: 87).

8 Organising the list of references

(a) (i)   Cable
   (ii) Brander and Spencer/Conrad
   (iii) Intriligator
   (iv) Gribben
   (v) *The Economist*
   (vi) OECD

(b) (i)   Author/Date/Title/Place of publication/Publisher
   (ii) Author(s)/Date/Article title/Journal title/Volume number/Page numbers
   (iii) Author(s)/Date/Chapter title/Editor(s)/Book title/Place of publication/Publisher
   (iv) URL of article/Date of access
   (v) Magazine title/URL of article/Access date or date of issue
   (vi) Name of organisation/Date/Title/Place of publication

(c) For book and journal titles

(d) For titles of books (not articles)

(e) Under the title of the publication

(f) (i)   (Brander and Spencer, 1985)
   (ii)   (Cable, 1983)
   (iii) (Conrad, 1989)
   (iv) (Gribben, 2009)
   (v)   (Intriligator, 2005)
   (vi) (OECD, 1998)
   (vii) (Runciman and Jenner, 2013)
   (viii) (*The Economist*, 2009)

1.8 Combining Sources

1 Mentioning sources

(a) 6
(b) Levels of technology anxiety
(c) Venkatesh
(d) Mick and Fournier
(e) 2

2 Taking a critical approach

(a) *Possible answer*:

Summary	Original
globalisation, although not a modern phenomenon . . .	globalisation is not a new phenomenon, but has its roots in the age of colonial development in the seventeenth and eighteenth centuries

(b) argues, emphasises, highlights
(c) However
(d) In contrast, Conversely

3 Practice

Model answer:

Lin (2006) demonstrates that globalisation has benefitted the multinationals, which have transferred production from countries with high labour costs to cheaper ones, whose workers thereby gain employment, while disadvantaging those where the facility has been lost. She also mentions the plight of the poorest nations, which have gained little from globalisation. Costa (2008) points out that the significant growth in international trade since 1990 has assisted many developing economies, such as the BRIC group. Brokaw (2002) examines the varying strategies of multinationals, which he claims have won substantial advantages from trade liberalisation.

4 Vocabulary revision

Simultaneously: At the same time
Ineptitude: Poor ability
Cross-border world trade: Buying and selling between counties
Outsourcing: Moving production or services abroad
Undoubtedly benefited: Certainly improved
Import tariff regimes: Tax on goods entering countries
Uniform quality: Regular standard
On the spot: Locally
Regional differences: Variations between areas
Tightly controlled: Strictly regulated

1.9 Organising Paragraphs

1 Paragraph structure

The answers are found below the table in section 2.

3 Practice A

(a) Topic sentence
Example
Reason
Supporting point 1
Supporting point 2
Supporting point 3

(b) for example/It is widely believed/In addition/But above all

(c) Despite this

4 Development of ideas

(a) Topic sentence   iv
Definition   ii
Result 1   i
Result 2   vi
Result 3   v
Conclusion   iii

(b) All these claims

(c) These/but/When this/Others/in other words/Even

6 Practice B

Model answer:

(a)

1 It has been argued that a rise in the rate of home ownership can increase the rate of unemployment.
2 This is because home ownership appears to make people more reluctant to move in order to find work.
3 Spain is an example of a country where high rates of home ownership coincide with high unemployment, while Switzerland demonstrates the opposite.
4 This theory, however, remains controversial.
5 It is clear that other factors, such as the liquidity of the housing market, must play a role in the relationship.

7 Practice C

Model answer:

Bill Gates was born in 1955, the second child in a middle-class Seattle family. He started writing computer programmes at the age of 13, and when he was 20 he set up a programming business with a school friend. In 1980, his company, called Microsoft, was asked to write an operating system by IBM for its new PC. Five years later, Microsoft launched the Windows operating system, and by 1995 Gates had become the richest man in the world. In 2006, he stepped down from running Microsoft to focus on his charitable foundation.

8 Vocabulary revision

(a) liquidity: liquid
reluctance: reluctant
stability: stable
prosperity: prosperous
controversy: controversial
conclusion: conclusive

(b) default: when a company or country is unable to pay its debts
sub-prime mortgage: loan to buy property to borrower with weak credit rating
housing bubble: unsustainable increase in property prices
income tax: tax paid on wages or salary
negative equity: owning an asset worth less than debt incurred to buy it

1.10 Introductions and Conclusions

1 Introduction contents

(a)

Components	Yes/No
(i) A definition of any unfamiliar terms in the title	Yes
(ii) The conclusions you reached on the topic	No
(iii) Mention of some sources you have read on the topic	Yes
(iv) A provocative idea or question to interest the reader	No
(v) Your aim or purpose in writing	Yes
(vi) The method you adopt to answer the question (or an outline)	Yes
(vii) Some background to the topic	Yes
(viii) Any limitations you set yourself	Yes

(b) (i) Purpose
(ii) Method
(iii) Definition
(iv) Limitation
(v) Outline
(vi) Background
(vii)Literature review

2 Introduction structure

Essential: Background/A review of some literature/Your purpose/Your method/Outline
Optional: Definitions/Limitations

3 Opening sentences

Model answers:

(a) In recent years, there has been steady criticism of the lack of women in senior management.
(b) The spectacular growth in international tourism in the last 40 years has been caused by several significant 'pull' factors.
(c) In the last 20 years, most Western economies have seen a steady decrease in inflation rates.
(d) Monopoly industries were a feature of the command economies of the communist bloc countries such as Czechoslovakia before 1990.

4 Practice A

Example introduction:

State control can be defined as meaning that industries are publicly financed, usually with ultimate control exercised by government ministers. Over the last two decades, there has been a global tendency to privatise many key industries that had formerly been in public ownership such as electricity and gas supply, railways and iron and steel production. There is continuing debate as to how far this process can continue; for example, some countries have privatised railways while in others they remain under state control.

This paper aims to evaluate the benefits and drawbacks of state control of industry. Using examples from the UK and France between 1990 and 2010, a comparison will be made of two key industries: electricity and railways. The first section will examine the benefits obtained from public ownership, then the disadvantages will be analysed. The final section will attempt to assess the limits of the privatisation process.

5 Conclusions

(a) Yes
(b) Yes
(c) No
(d) Yes
(e) Yes
(f) Yes
(g) Yes
(h) No
(i) f
(ii) b
(iii) e
(iv) d
(v) g
(vi) a

6 Practice B

Model conclusion:

Both social and economic benefits have been claimed for home ownership. But there is little strong evidence to support the arguments for economic advantages. Cultural factors may well account for the marked variations in home ownership across the developed world. It seems possible that high rates of ownership may contribute to unemployment by making people less willing to move, but further research is needed to establish whether this is significant. In such a short paper, the main issues can only be outlined, and clearly there may be social reasons for supporting wider home ownership, but the case for economic gains is harder to make.

1.11 Rewriting and Proofreading

2 Practice A

(a) Rather short (100 words) for introduction to a 2,000-word essay
(b) Some repetition of phrases and ideas (e.g. modern/today)
(c) No sources given for ideas (e.g. the inseparable relationship . . .)
(d) No specific mention of the motivation theories to be discussed
(e) No mention of which Japanese car producer will be focused on

3 Practice B

Issues:
No mention of Japanese company
Short sentences – more links needed to organise the discussion
Some repetition

Model conclusion:

It has been shown that the hierarchy of needs theory of Maslow, Herzberg's two-factor theory and the achievement theory of McClelland have some relevance to the motivation of British employees, and the application of these theories has sometimes resulted in increased employee performance. However, some limitations to the application of these theories have been demonstrated, using the experience of the Toyota Company in its British factories. Cross-cultural problems have arisen with regard to Japanese expectations and British attitudes to work. Furthermore, it appears that knowledge workers need different motivation methods, since the older theories of motivation are not always relevant to today's workplace, where a more up-to-date theoretical basis is needed.

4 Proofreading

(b) (i) Africa is not a country: *such as Nigeria*
    (ii) Innocence is a noun: *Young and innocent*
    (iii) Question mark needed: *What is the optimum size for a family business?*

    (iv) All verbs need to use past tense: *that produced*
    (vi) 'Successfulness' is not a word: *success*
    (vi) 'pervious' is incorrect: *previous*
    (vii) *One of the largest companies in Asia*
    (viii) Repetition: *the essay will conclude with an analysis of*
    (ix) Time periods need definite article: *the nineteenth century*
    (x) *when consumers go out shopping*

(c) (i) Style – use 'children'
    (ii) Singular/plural – their lines
    (iii) Vocabulary – torment is too strong, use 'inconvenience'
    (iv) Word ending – different effects
    (v) Factual – 1973
    (vi) Word order – overcome
    (vii) Punctuation – no comma needed
    (viii) Spelling – Hungary
    (ix) Missing word – the world
    (x) Tense: have entered

5 Practice C

<u>The</u> bicycle is one of <u>the</u> most efficient machine<u>s</u> ever designed. Cyclists can travel <u>four</u> times faster than walkers, <u>while</u> using less <u>energy</u> to do so. There were several early versions of the bicycle, but the first <u>model</u> with pedals which was successful<u>ly</u> mass-produced was <u>made</u> by a <u>F</u>renchman, Ernest Michaux, <u>in</u> 1861. Later <u>additions</u> included pneumatic tyres and gears. Today hundreds of <u>millions</u> of bicycles are in use all over <u>the</u> world.

1.12 Working in Groups

1 Group work

(a) False
(b) True
(c) False
(d) True
(e) True
(f) False

2 Making group work successful

1   Get to know the other members
2   Make everyone feel included
3   Analyse the task
4   Plan the job and responsibilities

5   Divide up the work fairly, according to the abilities of the members
6   Select a coordinator/editor
7   Finish the assignment on time

3 Dealing with problems

(a) (i)   The lazy students will learn nothing from this approach, and the same problem will occur next time they are involved in group work.
(ii)   Although it may seem difficult, this is the only positive solution.
(iii) Your teachers are unlikely to help – group work is designed to make these problems your responsibility.

(b) (i)   Your teachers are unlikely to help – group work is designed to make these problems your responsibility.
(ii)   This will not help you in the long run – you must learn to take part in discussion.
(iii) The right approach. The other members probably don't realise that you are having difficulties with their language.

(c) (i)   If everyone in the group takes part, the offender will be forced to accept that their behaviour is unhelpful.
(ii)   Your teachers are unlikely to help – group work is designed to make these problems your responsibility.
(iii) You will run the risk that they will get a poor mark and so everyone will suffer.

Revision Exercise: The Writing Process

Other answers may be possible.

(a) stage/part/step
(b) the/its
(c) for
(d) outline
(e) sources
(f) critically/rigorously/carefully
(g) which
(h) summarising
(i) answer
(j) draft
(k) avoid
(l) introduction
(m) After
(n) rewritten
(o) to
(p) list
(q) should/must
(r) proofread

Answers: Part 2

2.1 Argument and Discussion

1 Discussion vocabulary

(a) benefits/advantages
(b) drawbacks/disadvantages
(c) negative
(d) advantages/benefits
(e) disadvantages/drawbacks
(f) benefit/advantage

3 Practice A

Possible ideas include:

+	–
Saves commuting time	Employees may feel isolated
Gives employees more flexibility	May not suit all employees
Save expensive office space	Home may contain distractions
	Requires different management style

Model outline with structure (a)

(a) Introduction: reasons for growth home-working: development in communication technology, demand for more flexible work patterns.
(b) Drawbacks: employees may feel isolated, be distracted by activities at home, may not suit all employees, some prefer more direct management.
(c) Benefits: companies need to provide less office space, less time spent on commuting = more work time, employees have more flexibility.
(d) Discussion: of benefit to certain employees in some roles, but necessary to have regular contact with colleagues and managers.

5 Counterarguments

Model answers:

It has been claimed that employees may waste time at home, but in practice there seems little evidence for this.

Although homeworking may save companies money by reducing the need for office space, employees need to have a well-equipped workspace in their home.

6 Providing evidence

1   Drawbacks of imports – Inglehart
2   Benefits of imports – Indian case study (Goldberg *et al.*)
3   Writer's viewpoint

7 Practice B

Model answer:

It is widely thought that inflation is undesirable. Patterson (1998) points out that it can lead to industrial disputes as employees frequently demand pay rises to compensate for its effects, while excessive inflation results in lack of trust in money and uncertainty about the future. In contrast, Costa *et al.* (2012) demonstrate the advantages of moderate inflation in terms of stimulating spending and effectively reducing the value of debt. Clearly, the issue must be the level of inflation, and in practice most governments seem to encourage inflation levels of about 2%.

2.2 Cause and Effect

2 Practice A

Possible answers:

(a) Owing to the cold winter of 2013, there was increased demand for electricity.
(b) Tax cuts often lead to higher levels of spending.
(c) More people shopping on the internet may result in stores closing on the high street.
(d) The introduction of digital cameras resulted in reduced demand for photographic film.
(e) As a result of interest rates being increased last spring, there have been higher levels of saving.
(f) Falling sales of a firm's products can result in redundancies.
(g) Her aggressive managerial style caused an increase in labour disputes.

3 Practice B

Model answers:

(a) An increase in the tax on tobacco led to a fall in cigarette consumption.
(b) Rising demand for MBA courses led to tighter selection criteria being used.
(c) Lower fuel prices resulted in higher profits for freight companies.
(d) Bad weather in the Brazilian coffee-growing region caused a significant rise in coffee prices.
(e) The company's bankruptcy was due to careless accounting.
(f) The drop in share prices was caused by a steep rise in unemployment.
(g) Hiring extra staff was due to winning a new contract.
(h) A significant rise in profits was owing to the sharp depreciation of the dollar.

4 Practice C

(a) due to/owing to/produced by/because of/as a result of
(b) caused by/produced by/created by
(c) due to/because of/resulting from/caused by
(d) owing to/due to/because of
(e) lead to/cause/produce/result in/create
(f) results in/produces/causes/leads to
(g) results in/produces/causes/leads to

5 Practice D

Model paragraph:

An increase of 25% in the price of oil would have numerous results. First, it would lead to sharp rises in the cost of transport and freight, thus affecting the price of most goods. Clearly, businesses for which fuel was a significant proportion of their costs, such as airlines, would find it difficult to maintain profitability. Another consequence would be a reduction in oil consumption as marginal users switched to alternative fuels, such as gas, or made economies. There would also be increased investment in exploration for oil, as the oil companies attempted to increase supply, and this in turn would stimulate demand for equipment such as oil rigs. Finally, there would be a number of more localised effects, for instance a change in demand from larger to smaller and more economical vehicles.

2.3 Cohesion

2 Practice A

Reference	Reference word/phrase
La Ferrera	She
new businesses	they
average life of only 4.7 years	this
one economic	the former
one social	the latter
the former . . ., the latter . . .	these

4 Practice B

Velcro is a fabric fastener used with clothes and shoes. **It** was invented by a Swiss engineer called George de Mestral. **His** idea was derived from studying the tiny hooks found on some plant seeds. **They** cling to animals and help disperse the seeds. Velcro has two sides, one of which is covered in small hooks and the other in loops. When **they** are pressed together they form a strong bond.

Mestral spent eight years perfecting **his** invention, which **he** called 'Velcro' from the French words 'velour' and 'crochet'. **It** was patented in 1955 and today over 60 million metres of Velcro are sold annually.

5 Practice C

(a) He
(b) this/it
(c) It
(d) he
(e) them
(f) This
(g) his
(h) they
(i) he

6 Practice D

Model answer:

Wallace Carothers, the director of research at the American DuPont Corporation, invented nylon in 1935. He had previously studied chemistry, and specialised in polymers. They are molecules composed of long chains of atoms. Nylon is a strong but fine synthetic fibre which was first mass produced in 1939. It is used to make a wide range of products. These include stockings, toothbrushes, parachutes, fishing lines, and surgical thread.

2.4 Comparisons

2 Practice A

(a) Residential property in London is twice as expensive as in Rome.
(b) Property in Moscow is slightly cheaper than in New York.
(c) Tokyo property is nearly as expensive as property in Paris.
(d) Singapore has significantly cheaper property than New York.
(e) London is the most expensive of the eight cities, while Sydney is the cheapest.

Model answers:

(f) Parisian property is slightly cheaper than Moscow property.
(g) Property in Sydney is 50% cheaper than in New York.

5 Practice B

(a) Real Madrid was the richest club **in European football**.
(b) Real Madrid's income was almost twice **as** much as AC Milan's.
(c) FC Barcelona earned **significantly** more than Manchester City.
(d) Juventus had less revenue **than** Arsenal.
(e) Chelsea's income was **much** lower than Bayern Munich's.
(f) Manchester United earned approximately **the** same as Bayern Munich.

6 Practice C

(a) variations
(b) four
(c) as
(d) slightly
(e) than
(f) twice

7 Practice D

Model paragraph:

The table shows that Sainsbury's is a significantly larger company than Morrisons, with an annual turnover approximately 50% greater. The former has a market share of nearly 17%, while the latter's share is just over 12%. Sainsbury's has nearly 600 supermarkets, nearly 20% more than Morrisons, but the significant difference is in the number of convenience stores operated by each chain. While Sainsbury's has over 600, Morrisons only has 80. This may explain the huge difference in pre-tax profits: while Sainsbury's earned nearly £900 million, Morrisons recorded a loss of £176 million.

2.5 Definite Articles

4 Practice A

(a) Electrical engineering is the main industry in **the** northern region.
(b) Energy firms have made a record profit in **the** financial year 2012–2013.
(c) Global warming is partly caused by fossil fuels.
(d) **The** company's CEO has been arrested on fraud charges.
(e) Theft is costing **the** banking business millions of dollars a year.
(f) Tourism is **the** world's biggest industry.
(g) **The** forests of Scandinavia produce most of Britain's paper.
(h) **The** Thai currency is **the** baht.
(i) Computer crime has grown by 200% in **the** last decade.
(j) **The** main causes of **the** Industrial Revolution are still debated.
(k) Already 3% of **the** working population are employed in call centres.
(l) **The** latest forecast predicts rising unemployment for two years.
(m) Research on **the** housing market is being conducted in **the** business school.
(n) **The** best definition is often **the** simplest.

5 Practice B

(a) the/a
(b) –
(c) the/-
(d) –
(e) –
(f) the
(g) the
(h) the
(i) –
(j) an
(k) the
(l) the
(m) the
(n) –

2.6 Definitions

1 Simple definitions

(a) loan
(b) organisation
(c) period

(d) agreement
(e) costs
(f) financial instrument

Model answers:

(g) A trades union is an organisation of workers formed to protect its members' interests.
(h) A monopoly is a market in which one company has total or near-total control.
(i) Marketing is a process that focuses on identifying and satisfying consumer demand profitably.
(j) A dividend is a payment made by a company to its shareholders.
(k) A hostile takeover is the acquisition of a firm despite the opposition of its management board.

2 Complex definitions

(a) a failed project
(b) development
(c) electronic commerce
(d) corporate governance
(e) globalisation
(f) empathy
(i) a
(ii) c
(iii) f
(iv) b, d
(v) b, e

3 Practice

Model answers:

(a) **Managing diversity** policies are a systematic and comprehensive managerial process for developing an environment in which all employees, with their similarities and differences, can contribute to the organisation, and where no one is excluded due to unrelated factors.
(b) An **entrepreneurial business** is set up by somebody who demonstrates effective application of a number of enterprising attributes, such as creativity, initiative, risk taking, problem-solving ability, and autonomy, and will often risk his or her own capital.
(c) **Organisational culture** is a pattern of shared assumptions that the group learned as it solved its problems, which has proved itself and so is considered valid, and is passed on to new members.
(d) **Perfect competition** is characterised by a market so open that no participant can influence prices, without barriers to entry and with large numbers of buyers and sellers.

2.7 Examples

1 Using examples

(a) Illustration
(b) Support
(c) Support

2 Phrases to introduce examples

Model answers:

(a) Some twentieth-century inventions, such as TV and the internet, affected the lives of most people.
(b) A number of sports, for example motor racing, have become very profitable due to the sale of television rights.
(c) Various companies have built their reputation on the strength of one product, a case in point is Microsoft Windows.
(d) Some brands, for instance confectionery such as Mars bars, have remained successful for more than 50 years.
(e) In recent years, the product life cycle has tended to get shorter, particularly with electronic goods.
(f) A variety of products (e.g. shampoos) are promoted by celebrity endorsement.
(g) Speculation in some commodities, such as oil, has created price bubbles.
(h) Investors are often advised to spread their risk by putting their money into a range of investments, for instance equities, bonds and commodities.

3 Practice A

Model paragraph:

Widespread use of the internet has led to a major change in shopping habits. It is no longer necessary to visit shops to make routine purchases, **for example many supermarkets offer delivery services for online customers**. With more specialised items **such as books and music**, internet retailers can offer a wider range of products than bricks-and-mortar shops. They can also provide extra incentives to customers, **for instance free delivery or discounted prices**, in addition to the convenience of not having to visit a real shop. As a result, certain types of store (**e.g. bookshops**) are disappearing from the high street. Other products, however, **for instance clothing and footwear**, appear to require personal inspection and approval, and in addition many people enjoy the activity of shopping, so it seems unlikely that the internet will completely replace the shopping centre.

4 Practice B

Possible answers include:

Customs: holidays and festivals, ways of greeting people
Everyday patterns: types of shop, shop opening times
Inevitable differences: language, currency
Rapid changes of mood: depression, elation
Relatively short period: two/three months
Some aspects of their new surroundings: freedom, independence

5 Restatement

(a) The company's overheads, in other words the fixed costs, doubled last year.
(b) During a bear market, that is a period of falling share prices, few investors make money.
(c) The Indian capital, namely New Delhi, has a thriving commercial centre.
(d) The best-selling car of all time (i.e. the Toyota Corolla) has ceased production.

2.8 Generalisations

2 Structure

Model answers:

(b) Job satisfaction is not always related to the rate of pay.
(c) A weak currency tends to raise a country's level of exports.
(d) Spending on R&D is often linked to the introduction of new products.
(e) High rates of unemployment normally reduce the level of consumer spending.
(f) Cold weather is likely to increase demand for gas.

3 Overgeneralising

(a) Accurate
(b) Unemployment in 2009 was higher than in 1999 or 1989.
(c) Interest rates were lower in 2009 than in 1999 or 1989.
(d) Accurate

4 Practice

Model sentences:

(a) Most attempts to replicate Silicon Valley in other countries have failed.
(b) The reasons for Silicon Valley's success have not been understood.
(c) There are three ways in which such centres can grow.
(d) A recession can lead to the growth of new companies.
(e) A business-friendly culture is vital for success.

5 Building on generalisations

Example answer:

(a) In many countries, people tend to favour domestic products. Reasons for this preference include familiarity, patriotism and the fact that such products are often designed with local needs in mind. But with the growth of globalisation, domestic products are increasingly challenged by imported rivals.

2.9 Passives

2 Structure

(a) The data were collected and the two groups (were) compared.
(b) 120 people from six similar businesses were interviewed.
(c) The results were checked and several errors (were) found.
(d) An analysis of the findings will be made.
(e) Four managers were asked to give their opinions.
(f) The report was written and 10 copies (were) distributed.

3 Using adverbs

Other adverb combinations possible:

(a) The company was profitably run by the Connors family until 2001.
(b) The reasons for the Asian currency crisis were vigorously debated (by economists).
(c) All students in the exam were helpfully provided with pencils.
(d) A presentation was vividly given by the staff of the advertising agency.
(e) The percentages were accurately calculated to three decimal places (by researchers).
(f) Their business was optimistically called the Grand Universal Trading Company.
(g) The life cycles of over 240 companies were carefully researched.

5 Practice B

Passive	Active possible?	Active
He was worn out	Yes	The effort . . . had worn him out
He was born	No	
John was concerned by	Yes	The situation of the poor concerned John . . .
a (. . .) shop which was called	Yes	which he called
the business was taken over	Yes	his wife took the business over
she was soon assisted	Yes	their 10-year-old son assisted her

The effect of using the passive throughout would be to make the tone very formal.

6 Practice C

Model paragraph:

In 1889 he was introduced to Florence Rowe, the daughter of a bookseller, while on holiday. After they were married her ideas affected the business: the product range was enlarged to include stationery and books. The Boots subscription library and in-store cafes were also introduced due to Florence's influence. During World War I the Boots factories made a variety of products, from sterilisers to gas masks. But after the war Jesse was attacked by arthritis and, worried by the economic prospects, he sold the company to an American rival for £2m. This, however, went bankrupt during the Depression and Boots was then bought by a British group for £6m, and Jesse's son, John, became chairman. The famous No.7 cosmetics range was launched in the 1930s and in World War II the factories produced both saccharin and penicillin. However, recently the company has been threatened by intense competition from supermarkets in its core pharmaceutical business.

2.10 Problems and Solutions

3 Practice A

Problem	Many developing countries have found that the development of a tourism industry can bring social and environmental drawbacks . . .
Solution A	One possible solution is to target upmarket holidaymakers, in order to get the maximum profit from minimum numbers.
Argument against solution A	However, this is a limited market and requires considerable investment in infrastructure and training.
Solution B	Another remedy is to rigorously control the environmental standards of any development, in order to minimise the impact of the construction.
Conclusion in favour of B	This requires effective government agencies, but is likely to ensure the best outcome for both tourists and locals.

5 Practice B

Model argument:

Currently there is increasing demand for university places, which frequently leads to overcrowding of teaching situations. It has been argued that fees should be increased to reduce demand for places, but this would discriminate against students from poorer families. Another proposal is for the government to pay for the expansion of universities, but against this is the view that this would unfairly benefit the minority who in any case go on to earn higher salaries. A fairer solution might be for the government to subsidise the fees of the poorest students.

2.11 Punctuation

9 Practice A

(a) The study was carried out by Christine Zhen-Wei Qiang of the World Bank.

(b) Professor Rowan's new book 'The Triumph of Capitalism' is published in New York.
or
Professor Rowan's new book *The Triumph of Capitalism* is published in New York.

(c) As Keynes said: 'It's better to be roughly right than precisely wrong.'

(d) Three departments, Law, Business and Economics, have had their funding cut.

(e) As Cammack (1994) points out: 'Latin America is creating a new phenomenon; democracy without citizens.'

(f) Thousands of new words such as 'app' enter the English language each year.

(g) In 2005, France's per-capita GDP was 73% of America's.

(h) She scored 56% on the main course; the previous semester she had achieved 67%.

10 Practice B

The London School of Business is offering three new courses this year: Economics with Psychology, Introduction to Management and e-commerce. The first is taught by Dr Jennifer Hillary and runs from October to January. The second, Introduction to Management, for MSc. Finance students is offered in the second semester, and is assessed by coursework only. Professor Wang's course in e-commerce runs in both the autumn and the spring, and is for more experienced students.

2.12 Singular or Plural?

1 Five areas of difficulty

(a) . . . and disadvantages (v)

(b) are under 30 (i)

(c) rural areas (iii)

(d) . . . in crime (ii)

(e) Each company has its own policy (iv)

4 Practice A

(a) Little

(b) businesses

(c) experience/is

(d) travel broadens

(e) much advice

(f) few interests

(g) civil war
(h) irons were
(i) work

5 Practice B

companies have/websites/e-commerce/this is/businesses/their/trouble/security/expense/mean/these companies

2.13 Style

3 Practice A

Model sentences:

(a) The main factor in the collapse of Lehman Brothers was . . .
(b) There appears to be a significant risk of inflation increasing.
(c) It is commonly believed that the economy is deteriorating.
(d) After 1989, the price of Japanese property fell sharply.
(e) The numbers in that report are unreliable.
(f) The German inflation led to poverty and social unrest.
(g) The manager was dismissed for embezzlement.
(h) Currently there is high unemployment.

4 Avoiding repetition and redundancy

Model answer:

Currently, fast food is growing in popularity. Fast food is food that people can buy or cook quickly. This essay examines the advantages and drawbacks of fast food. First, it is usually tasty. Most people who work in offices are very busy, so they do not have time to go home for lunch. But they can eat tasty food in restaurants such as McDonald's. The second benefit of fast food is cheapness. As it is produced in large quantities, this means that companies can keep costs down. As a result it is usually less expensive than a meal in a conventional restaurant.

5 Varying sentence length

Model answers:

Worldwide, enrolments in higher education are increasing. In developed countries, over half of all young people enter college, while similar trends are seen in China and South America. This growth has put financial strain on state university systems, so that many countries are asking students and parents to contribute. This leads to a debate about whether students or society benefit from tertiary education.

China is one developing country (but not the only one) that has imposed fees on students since 1997. The results have been surprising: enrolments, especially in the most expensive universities, have continued to rise steeply, growing 200% overall between 1997 and 2011. It seems in this case that higher fees attract rather than discourage students, who see them as a sign of a good education. They compete more fiercely for places, leading to the result that a place at a good college can cost $8,000 per year for fees and maintenance.

6 The use of caution

Others are possible:

Modals: might/may/could/should
Adverbs: often/usually/frequently/generally/mainly
Verb/phrase: seems to/appears to/in general/by and large/it appears/it seems

7 Using modifiers

(a) The company's efforts to save energy were quite/fairly successful.
(b) The survey was (a fairly/quite a) comprehensive study of student opinion.
(c) His second book had a rather hostile reception.
(d) The first year students were quite fascinated by her lectures.
(e) The latest type of mobile phone is rather expensive.

8 Practice B

Model answers:

(a) Private companies are often more efficient than state-owned businesses.
(b) Exploring space may be a waste of valuable resources.
(c) Older students tend to perform better at university than younger ones.
(d) Word-of-mouth is commonly the best kind of advertising.
(e) English pronunciation can be confusing.
(f) Most shopping may done on the internet in ten years' time.

2.14 Visual Information

1 Types of visuals

TYPES	USES	EXAMPLE
1 Diagram	d	E
2 Table	f	B
3 Map	a	F
4 Pie chart	c	D
5 Bar chart	b	C
6 Line graph	e	A

2 The language of change

Others possible:

(a) rose/increased
(b) levelled off
(c) steadily
(d) rose/increased
(e) slightly
(f) climbed/rose
(g) peak
(h) dropped/fell
(i) sharply/steeply

3 Describing visuals

(a) (i) is better. It comments on the main features of the chart but does not repeat the statistics.
(b) *Model answers:*

(a) density
(b) demonstrates/illustrates
(c) between
(d) less-crowded/less densely populated
(e) role/part
(f) since/as/because
(g) tend

5 Practice A

Model answers:

(a) shows
(b) French
(c) figure
(d) countries/states
(e) than
(f) higher

6 Practice B

Model paragraph:

Table 2 shows the world's ten largest companies by revenue in 2013. It is noticeable that seven of the ten, including the second and third largest are oil companies. The largest company, Wal-Mart, is a multinational retailer, and the eighth, Vitol, is a commodity trader.

Revision Exercise: Elements of Writing

1 drawback/negative factor or aspect/con or minus (informal)

2 It is widely considered that the traditional high street shop is becoming redundant.

3 *State-owned companies are often seen as inefficient*, but certain industries do involve a 'natural monopoly'.

4 *Example sentences:*

   The increase in house prices is due to rising demand for housing.
   Rising demand for housing leads to an increase in house prices.

5 The Rolls-Royce Company   It
   Henry Royce   The former
   Charles Rolls   the latter
   Henry Royce and Charles Rolls   Their/they

6 *Model sentences:*

   A Rolls Royce car is much more expensive than a Toyota Prius.
   A Toyota Prius is far more economical than a Rolls Royce car.
   The Toyota Prius is more popular than a Rolls Royce.

7 See page 110

8 (a) A graduate is a person who has gained a first degree at a university.
   (b) A scholarship is a sum of money awarded to a student to allow him or her to study.
   (c) A limited company is a business whose owners' liability for losses is restricted to their investment.

9 *Example sentences:*

   (a) A few districts such as Silicon Valley are famous for technological innovation.
   (b) Certain inventions, for instance mobile phones, have changed the way we live.
   (c) Some successful entrepreneurs have had little formal business education, a case in point is Richard Branson.

10 (a) With the plural: Middle managers are under threat.
   (b) Using 'the' + singular: The middle manager is under threat.

11 Google was begun in 1996 as a research project by Page and Brin. (passive)
   Page and Brin began Google as a research project in 1996. (active)

12 The twenty-first century has seen the rise of the BRIC economies: Brazil, Russia, India and China. The acronym was first used in a paper written by Jim O'Neill in 2001.

13 To be objective, accurate and impersonal.

14 (a) changes in time (b) function (c) proportion (d) statistical display

Answers: Part 3

3.1 Approaches to Vocabulary

2 Discussing language

Examples are provided in section 3.

3 Practice

(b) statement
(c) anecdote
(d) saying
(e) euphemism
(f) metaphor
(g) understatement
(h) paradox
(i) simile
(j) proverb
(k) synopsis
(m) slogan
(n) ambiguity
(o) cliché

4 Confusing pairs

(a) principles
(b) lose
(c) affect
(d) compliments
(e) economic
(f) accepted

3.2 Abbreviations

6 Practice

(a) information and communications technology/State-owned enterprises/and others
(b) unique selling point
(c) that is/World Trade Organisation
(d) note/curricula vitae/Human Resources
(e) Organisation for Economic and Cultural Development/United Arab Emirates
(f) European Union/Value Added Tax
(g) Chief Executive Officer/Research and Development
(h) Figure 4/world wide web
(i) British Airways/Hong Kong/Kuala Lumpur
(j) Public relations/approximately/$75,000
(k) With reference to/Annual General Meeting/as soon as possible
(l) Professor/Master of Science/Doctor of Philosophy

3.3 Academic Vocabulary: Nouns and Adjectives

1 Nouns

NB: Not all these words have close synonyms. This list is a guide to approximate meaning. Students should use a dictionary for a full understanding.

accuracy – precision
analysis – examination
approach – angle of study
assessment – test
assumption – informed guess
authority – expert
category – type
claim – argument
controversy – debate
correlation – link
deterrent – disincentive
emphasis – weight put on one area
evidence – proof
exception – different thing
extract – part of a longer work
ideology – belief
implication – unstated suggestion
innovation – new introduction
intuition – understanding without thinking
motivation – incentive

perspective – angle of study
phenomenon – unusual event
policy – formal guidelines
preference – favourite choice
process – series of stages
proposal – suggestion
provision – supply
sequence – series of stages
strategy – plan
substitute – replacement
technique – method
validity – truth

(a) evidence
(b) suggestions
(c) intuition
(d) provision
(e) correlation

2 Using nouns and adjectives

Noun	Adjective	Noun	Adjective
approximation	approximate	particularity	particular
superiority	superior	reason	reasonable
strategy	strategic	synthesis	synthetic
politics	political	economy	economic/al
industry	industrial	culture	cultural
exterior	external	average	average
height	high	reliability	reliable
heat	hot	strength	strong
confidence	confident	truth	true
width	wide	probability	probable
necessity	necessary	length	long
danger	dangerous	relevance	relevant

3 Practice A

Others may be possible

(a) confident
(b) particularities/strengths
(c) probability

(d) relevant

(e) necessary

(f) average

(g) danger

(h) necessity

(i) unreliable

(j) approximate

(k) economic

(l) synthesis

5 Practice B

(a) irrelevant

(b) subjective/irrational

(c) Concrete/Relevant

(d) approximate/rough

(e) relative

(f) logical/rational

(g) theoretical/abstract

(h) unambiguous

6 Practice C

(a) strategic – strategy

(b) analytical – analysis

(c) synthetic – synthesis

(d) major – majority

(e) cultural – culture

(f) theoretical – theory

(g) frequent – frequency

(h) critical – criticism/critic

(i) social – society

(j) practical – practice

3.4 Academic Vocabulary: Verbs and Adverbs

1 Understanding main verbs

NB: Approximate synonyms

arise = occur

conduct = carry out

characterise = have features of

clarify = explain
concentrate on = look at closely
be concerned with = deal with
demonstrate = show
determine = find
discriminate = distinguish
establish = found
exhibit = show
focus on = look at closely
generate = create
hold = be true
identify = pick out
imply = suggest
interact = work together
interpret = explain
manifest = show
overcome = defeat
propose = suggest
prove = turn out
recognise = accept
relate to = link to
supplement = add to
undergo = experience
yield = produce

3 Practice A

Other verbs may be possible

(a) A admitted/accepted that he might have made a mistake . . .
(b) B denied saying that women make better economists than men.
(c) C stated/claimed/argued that small firms are more dynamic than large ones.
(d) D agreed with C's views on small firms.
(e) E assumed/presumed that most people work for money.
(f) F concluded that growing wheat is more profitable than growing potatoes.
(g) G doubted that electric cars would replace conventional ones.
(h) H hypothesised/suggested a link between age and entrepreneurial ability.

5 Practice B

Other verbs may be possible

(a) L criticised/censured her research methods.
(b) M identified/classified four main types of government bonds.
(c) N commended the company for its record for workplace safety.

(d) O interpreted falling unemployment as a sign of economic recovery.
(e) P identified/presented wind power and biomass as the leading green energy sources.
(f) Q described/portrayed Adam Smith as the most influential economist of the eighteenth century.

7 Practice C

Others are possible

(a) particularly
(b) Originally
(c) Alternatively
(d) Recently
(e) locally
(f) Clearly/Crucially

3.5 Conjunctions

1 Types of conjunctions

(a) A few inventions, <u>for instance</u> television, have had a major impact on everyday life.
(b) <u>In addition</u>, a large volume of used cars are sold through dealerships.
(c) The definition of motivation is important <u>since</u> it is the cause of some disagreement.
(d) The technology allows consumers a choice, <u>thus</u> increasing their sense of satisfaction.
(e) Four hundred people were interviewed for the survey, <u>then</u> the results were analysed.
(f) <u>However</u>, another body of opinion associates globalisation with unfavourable outcomes.
(ii) d
(iii) c
(iv) f
(v) a
(vi) e

2 Practice A

Conjunction	Type	Conjunction	Type
(a) such as	example	(f) in other words	example
(b) but	opposition	(g) instead of	opposition
(c) Although	opposition	(h) Consequently	result
(d) for instance	example	(i) and	addition
(e) however	opposition	(j) neither . . . nor	opposition

3 Common conjunctions

Others are possible

Addition: moreover/as well as/in addition/and/also/furthermore
Result: therefore/consequently/so/that is why (see Unit 2.2 Cause and Effect)
Reason: because/owing to/as a result of/as/since/due to (see Unit 2.2 Cause and Effect)
Time: after/while/then/next/subsequently (see Unit 3.10 Time Markers)
Example: such as/e.g./in particular/for instance (see Unit 2.7 Examples)
Opposition: but/yet/while/however/nevertheless/whereas/albeit/although/despite

4 Practice B

Others are possible

(a) After
(b) Although/While
(c) moreover/furthermore/additionally
(d) therefore/so
(e) for instance/for example
(f) Due to/Because of
(g) While
(h) As/Because/Since

5 Conjunctions of opposition

Model answers:

(a) (i) Although the government claimed that inflation was falling, the opposition said it was rising.
    (ii) The government claimed that inflation was falling while the opposition said it was rising.

(b) (i) This department must reduce expenditure, yet it needs to install new computers.
    (ii) While this department must reduce expenditure, it also needs to install new computers.

(c) (i) In spite of being heavily advertised, sales of the new car were poor.
    (ii) Sales of the new car were poor despite being heavily advertised.

6 Practice C

Model answers:

(a) In contrast to America, where car ownership is widespread, few Liberians have cars.
(b) Despite leaving school at the age of 14, he went on to develop a successful business.
(c) The majority displayed a positive attitude to the proposal, but a minority strongly disagreed.

(d) While the tutor insisted that the essay was easy, the students found it difficult.

(e) Although the spring was cold and dry, the summer was warm and wet.

(f) Nobody expected the restaurant to succeed, yet it was full every evening.

3.6 Numbers

2 Percentages

(a) 50%

(b) 100%

(c) 400%

3 Simplification

(b) Scores of students applied for the scholarship.

(c) He rewrote the essay several/a few times.

(d) Dozens of books were published on the economic crisis.

(e) Various names were suggested, but rejected, for the new chocolate bar.

4 Further numerical phrases

Model answers:

(a) The price of petrol has increased tenfold since 1975.

(b) Two-thirds of the students in the group were Japanese.

(c) The new high-speed train halved the journey time to Madrid.

(d) The number of students applying for the Management course has risen by 50%.

(e) The number of visitors to the theme park doubled every year from 2012 to 2014.

(f) More than twice as many British students as Italian students complete their first degree course.

(g) Tap water is 700 times cheaper than bottled water.

(h) The highest rate of unemployment is in Spain and the lowest in Norway.

(i) 27% of the garments produced had some kind of fault.

(j) A majority of shareholders supported the proposal, but a large proportion of these expressed some doubts.

5 Practice

Model answers:

(b) Management was the most popular future course.

(c) One-fifth of the group planned to study Economics.

(d) Only one student was over 23.

(e) Swimming was the favourite sport of one-third of the group.

(f) The least popular sports were cycling and tennis.

3.7 Prefixes and Suffixes

2 Prefixes

auto	by itself
co	together
ex	(i) previous
	(ii) outside
fore	in front
inter	between
macro	large
micro	small
multi	many
over	too much
poly	many
post	later
re	again
sub	below
trans	across
under	(i) below
	(ii) not enough

3 Practice A

(a) social class at bottom of society
(b) more tickets sold than seats available
(c) very local climate
(d) economy based on information not production
(e) not listed in the telephone directory
(f) disappointed

5 Practice B

(a) noun – withdrawal of a service
(b) adjective – two related events at the same time
(c) adverb – without cooperation
(d) adjective – related to evolution
(e) noun – person who protests
(f) adjective – not able to be forecast
(g) adjective – able to be sold
(h) noun – person being interviewed
(i) noun – belief that increasing consumption benefits society
(j) adverb – in a way that suggests a symbol

6 Practice C

(a) joint production/junior company
(b) without choosing to/not hurt
(c) able to be refilled/clear and obvious
(d) cannot be provided/unusual
(e) failure in communication/new order

3.8 Prepositions

1 Using prepositions

purpose of/development of/in Catalonia/over the period/contributed to/valuable for/In conclusion/ sets out/relationship between/decline in/supply of/in the factory context

Verb + = contributed to
Adj + = valuable for
Phrasal verb = sets out
Place = in Catalonia/in the factory context
Time = over the period
Phrase = In conclusion

2 Practice A

(b) adjective +
(c) verb +
(d) preposition of place
(e) noun +
(f) phrase
(g) preposition of place
(h) preposition of time

3 Prepositions and nouns

(a) of
(b) in
(c) of
(d) to
(e) in
(f) on

4 Prepositions in phrases

(a) on
(b) of
(c) of
(d) in
(e) in
(f) on
(g) in
(h) of

5 Prepositions of place and time

(a) Among
(b) from, to/between, and
(c) in, of
(d) in, in
(e) in, at
(f) On, between
(g) of, on

6 Practice B

(a) out
(b) of
(c) in/to
(d) to
(e) among/in
(f) from/in
(g) between
(h) in
(i) of
(j) in/over
(k) between
(l) in
(m) in
(n) of
(o) to/in

8 Practice C

(a) focused on/concentrated on
(b) pointed out
(c) specialising in

(d) associated with
(e) divided into
(f) blamed for
(g) believed in

3.9 Synonyms

1 How synonyms work

Word/phrase	Synonym
largest	giant
oil	hydrocarbon
company	firm
in the world	global/internationally
people	employees

2 Common synonyms in academic writing

NB: These pairs are not synonymous in every situation.

Nouns		Verbs	
area	field	accelerate	speed up
authority	source	achieve	reach
behaviour	conduct	alter	change
beliefs	ethics	analyse	take apart
benefit	advantage	assist	help
category	type	attach	join
component	part	challenge	question
concept	idea	claim	suggest
controversy	argument	clarify	explain
drawback	disadvantage	concentrate on	focus on
expansion	increase	confine	limit
feeling	emotion	develop	evolve
framework	structure	eliminate	remove
goal	target	evaluate	examine
hypothesis	theory	found	establish
interpretation	explanation	maintain	insist

issue	topic	predict	forecast
method	system	prohibit	ban
option	possibility	quote	cite
quotation	citation	raise	increase
results	findings	reduce	decrease
statistics	figures	respond	reply
study	research	retain	keep
trend	tendency	show	demonstrate
output	production	strengthen	reinforce

3 Practice A

Model answers:

(a) Professor Hicks <u>challenged</u> the <u>results</u> of the <u>study</u>.
(b) The <u>figures</u> <u>demonstrate</u> a steady <u>rise</u> in student numbers.
(c) The institute's <u>forecast</u> has caused a major <u>debate</u>.
(d) Cost seems to be the <u>principal</u> <u>disadvantage</u> to that <u>method</u>.
(e) They will <u>focus</u> <u>on</u> the first <u>possibility</u>.
(f) During the lecture, she tried to <u>explain</u> her <u>theory</u>.
(g) Three <u>topics</u> need to be <u>evaluated</u>.
(h) The <u>structure</u> can be <u>kept</u> but the <u>aim</u> needs to be <u>modified</u>.
(i) OPEC, the oil producers' cartel, is to <u>reduce</u> <u>output</u> to <u>increase</u> global prices.
(j) The <u>tendency</u> to smaller families has <u>accelerated</u> in the last decade.

4 Practice B

UK – British – this country
agency – organisation – body
advertising campaign – publicity programme – advertising blitz
to raise – to improve
to cut – reduction
before eating – prior to meals

5 Practice C

Model answers:

build/make vehicles
car makers
principal problem
obstacle
automobile producers
challenges
forecast

3.10 Time Markers

3 Practice A

(a) Recently
(b) until
(c) for
(d) Last month
(e) by
(f) Since
(g) During

4 Practice B

(a) Last
(b) During/On
(c) By
(d) for
(e) ago
(f) later
(g) until
(h) Currently/Now

5 Practice C

(a) In/Over
(b) Since
(c) ago
(d) recently
(e) Currently
(f) by
(g) since

6 Practice D

(a) until
(b) later
(c) after/in
(d) During
(e) By/In
(f) for
(g) since
(h) after
(i) until/into
(j) before

Answers: Part 4

4.1 Case Studies

1 Using case studies

A case study has the advantage of providing a concrete experience/example.

The disadvantage is that it is limited in place and time.

Topics	Case studies
Improving crop yields in semi-deserts	Using solar power to operate irrigation pumps in Ethiopia
Encouraging entrepreneurship in Africa	A Moroccan scheme for subsidising new business start-ups
Improving recycling rates in large cities	The Berlin experiment: increasing public participation in collecting and sorting waste
The impact of the housing market on the wider economy	The effect of the 2008 property crash on Spanish banking
Approaches to motivation in the service sector	A study of a French supermarket training programme
Making health care more cost-effective	Using the internet to reduce visits to the doctor in Dublin

2 Model case study

Additional answers are possible here

(a) Store layouts match Chinese apartments
Products linked to New Year celebrations

Reduced prices by sourcing production locally
Produces thinner but more frequent catalogues
Uses local characters in adverts
Attempts to provide better service

(b) Competition from rivals offering free delivery
Some products (e.g. single beds) not suited to Chinese tastes

(c) More financial details of IKEA's sales and profits in the Chinese market

4.2 Formal Letters and Emails

1 Letters

(a) Address of sender
(b) Address of recipient
(c) Sender's reference
(d) Date
(e) Greeting
(f) Subject headline
(g) Reason for writing
(h) Further details
(i) Request for response
(j) Ending
(k) Signature
(l) Sender's name and job title

Model reply:

---

54 Sydney Road
Rowborough RB1 6FD

Mr M. Bramble
Administrative Assistant
Central Admissions Office
Wye House
Park Campus
University of Mercia
Borchester BR3 5HT

5th May 2014

Dear Mr Bramble,

Informal Interview: Yr Ref: MB/373

Thank you for inviting me to interview on May 21st. I will be able to attend on that date, but it would be much more convenient if I could have the interview at 12, due to the train times from Rowborough.

Could you please let me know if this alteration is possible?

Yours sincerely,

P. Tan

P. Tan

---

3 Practice

Sender = student/recipient = teacher
Reply is unlikely, unless recipient needs to comment on the attached paper.

Model answers:

(a) Hi Mark,
    We need to schedule a short meeting tomorrow. What time would suit you?
    See you soon,

(b) Hello Tricia,
    I'm looking for another source for this month's essay. Could you recommend something suitable?
    Best wishes,

(c) Hi everyone,
    It's only a week before the end of the course – what are we going to do to celebrate? Let me have your ideas – I'll pass them on and hopefully get something good fixed up for Sat 12th!

(d) Dear Tim Carey,
    I've never had this book, so I can't return it. Can you check your records please?

4.3 Literature Reviews

2 Example literature review

(a) 2 (content & process)
(b) 7
(c) 5
(d) It is more convenient to use secondary sources in this kind of short literature review. If you were studying just one of these theorists (e.g. Herzberg), you might be expected to use primary sources.

4.5 Reports

2 Essays and reports

1   Essay
2   Report
3   Report
4   Report/essay
5   Essay

3 Practice

Introduction

(e)
(b)
(d)
(c)
(a)

Example report

Proposals

The central feature of Plan A is a circular park area in the middle of the site, which would contain trees and seating. On one side of this is a small car park, with space for 20 vehicles. On the other side is a block of tennis courts. The alternative, Plan B, provides a larger car park along the side next to the Access Road, with spaces for 50 cars. The other half of the site contains a building housing a café and a range of shops at one end, while at the other end is a swimming pool.

Discussion

Clearly, the two proposals offer quite different amenities. Plan A provides some green space for relaxation, along with tennis courts and a limited amount of parking. It is a relatively low-key scheme that could be completed quite cheaply. In contrast, Plan B would be more expensive, but would also offer catering and sporting facilities as well as extra parking.

Recommendations

It can be argued in favour of Plan B that a swimming pool would have wider appeal than tennis courts, and also that there is a severe shortage of parking on the campus. However, it is not clear that more shops and a café are really needed for the university, and few students actually drive cars. Plan A would also do more to improve the look of the campus by increasing the green space. In view of these considerations, the university should perhaps consider combining the best of both plans, and replace the tennis courts in Plan A with a swimming pool.

4.6 Surveys

1 Conducting surveys

Other suggestions possible/in any order

Get up-to-date data
Collect information about the behaviour of a specific group (e.g. clients of a firm)
Test a hypothesis

2 Questionnaire design

(a) (ii) is less embarrassing for most people to answer.
(b) (i) is an open question and has many possible answers.
    (ii) is a closed question with a limited range of responses.
(c) For casual interviews, ten is probably the maximum most interviewees will cope with.

3 Survey language

(a) conducted
(b) random
(c) questionnaire
(d) questioned
(e) respondents/interviewees
(f) interviewees/respondents
(g) mentioned
(h) majority
(i) slightly
(j) minority
(k) questions
(l) common
(m) generally
(n) sample

4 Question forms

Model questions. 3–6 could use present tense.

Q2: Why did you take a job?
Q3: What effect did the work have on your studies?
Q4: What kind of work did you do?
Q5: What hours did you work?
Q6: How much did you earn?
Q7: Do you have any comments on your work?

5 Tenses

(a) past tense
(b) present tense (the survey is completed but the results are still valid)

Revision Exercise: Taking Ideas from Sources

(e) *Model notes:*

(i) Happiness often depends on feeling wealthier than others.
(ii) People believe that leisure = happiness, so working longer to get extra goods won't lead to happiness.

(f) *Model answer:*

Another explanation Penec presents is that happiness is often dependent on a comparison with others, so that if neighbours are also getting richer, there is no apparent improvement. A further factor relates to leisure, which is widely equated with happiness. Consequently, the idea of increasing workload to be able to purchase more goods or services is not going to result in greater happiness.

(g) Penec, A. (2008) 'The measurement of happiness' *Applied Econometrics* 44, pp. 18–27.

Glossary

Abbreviation	The short form of a word or phrase (see Unit 3.2)
Abstract	A short summary of the aims and scope of a journal article (see Unit 1.2)
Acknowledgements	A list of people the author wishes to thank for their assistance, found in books and articles
Appendix (plural – appendices)	A section at the end of a book or article containing supplementary information
Assignment	A task given to students, normally for assessment
Authority	A well-known expert on a subject
Back issue	A previous issue of a journal or magazine
Bias	A subjective preference for one point of view
Bibliography	A list of sources an author has read but not specifically cited
Brainstorm	A process of collecting ideas on a topic at random (see Unit 1.4)
Case study	A section of an essay that examines one example in detail (see Unit 4.1)
Citation	An in-text reference providing a link to the source (see Units 1.3 and 1.7)
Cohesion	Linking ideas in a text together by use of reference words (see Unit 2.3)
Coursework	Assessed assignments given to students to complete during a course

Conclusion	The final section of an essay or report (see Unit 1.10)
Contraction	A shortened form (e.g. she's, I'd)
Criteria (singular – criterion)	The principles on which something is judged or based
Deadline	The final date for completing a piece of work
Draft	The first attempt at a piece of writing
Edited book	A book with contributions from a number of writers, controlled by an editor
Extract	A piece of text taken from a longer work
Flow chart	Diagram that illustrates the stages of a process
Formality	In written work, the use of a non-idiomatic style and vocabulary
Format	The standard pattern of layout for a text
Heading	The title of a section of text
Higher degree	A Master's degree or Doctorate
Hypothesis	A theory that a researcher is attempting to explore/test
Introduction	The first part of an essay or article (see Unit 1.10)
Journal	An academic publication in a specialised area, usually published quarterly (see Unit 1.2)
Literature review	A section of an article describing other research on the topic in question (see Unit 4.3)
Main body	The principal part of an essay, after the introduction and before the conclusion
Margin	The strip of white space on a page around the text
Module	Most academic courses are divided into modules, which examine a specified topic
Outline	A preparatory plan for a piece of writing (see Unit 1.4)
Paraphrase	A rewriting of a text with substantially different wording and organisation but similar ideas
Peer-review	The process of collecting comment from academic authorities on an article before publication in a journal; this system gives increased validity to the publication
Phrase	A few words that are commonly combined (see Unit 1.1)

Plagiarism	Using another writer's work without proper acknowledgement (see Unit 1.3)
Primary research	Original research (e.g. a study of how a business functions)
Quotation	Use of the exact words of another writer to illustrate your writing (see Unit 1.7)
Redundancy	The unnecessary repetition of ideas or information (see Unit 2.13)
References	A list of all the sources you have cited in your work (see Unit 1.7)
Register	The level of formality in language
Restatement	Repeating a point in order to explain it more clearly
Scan	A method of reading in which the eyes move quickly over the page to find a specific item
Skim	A related reading technique to quickly find out the main ideas of a text
Source	The original text you have used to obtain an idea or piece of information
Summary	A shorter version of something (see Unit 1.6)
Synonym	A word or phrase with a similar meaning to another (see Unit 3.9)
Synopsis	A summary of an article or book
Term	Word or phrase used to express a special concept
Word class	A grammatical category (e.g. noun, adjective)

Index